Book One

On *Extinctions*

'The "vignettes" in *Extinctions* challenge, again, what I think I understand about, and have come to expect from short pieces of prose. They lie, as so much of Mohanty's work does, in the spaces in-between – in between prose and poetry, fiction and non-fiction, telling and showing, image and word, poem and prayer.'

Janice Pariat in *Scroll*

'Sharmistha Mohanty's works have always been characterized by a certain largesse, a ceaseless seeking to incorporate in her writing that which lies between and beyond words, to constantly explore and push the boundaries of how one experiences and creates literature. *Extinctions*, like her other books, assumes a similar in-between status, hovering somewhere between poetry and prose, fiction and non-fiction, and literature and philosophy.

'Much of *Extinction*'s power lies in Sharmistha's spare and elemental handling of the English language, resulting in passages of astonishing intensity.'

Vedant Srinivas in *The Los Angeles Review*

On *The Gods Came Afterwards*

'In *The Gods Came Afterwards*, Sharmistha Mohanty has created a stunning sequence of songs of quest and aspiration, moving through multiple states of mind and "remains of melted meteorites". There is a charged authority here, a forceful lyrical evocation of contemplative power and urgency. We are back in a primal world that has been lost or abused and yet these songs are present, here, now, in our "injured evening", our "scarred forests" with the terror of the owl screeching above us losing a wing, or the falling bricks of a metaphorical falcon. I think of our falling and failing cities, our need for wisdom, guidance, ritual, our need to heal and "calm the anxiety in our hands" which conjures our fraught cell device addiction. Inspired in part by the Rig Veda, the poet reanimates the "voice" of magical sacred text with agency, with sparks of spare simplicity, with skill and devotion. The call for relief in these poems is unforgettable. Have the gods come after? Have they been cast aside? Are we still waiting? Or are we back before them in our existential oracular relationship with Nature? This book is a haunting meditation. We are both "very far very far" and "very near very near" with "astral distance wedged in the spinal cord".'

Anne Waldman

On *Five Movements in Praise*

'Sharmistha Mohanty is a clear and present example of the writer as caver, her work a descent into rock in pursuit of a shape half known and calling. It's not surprising that her touchstone is the great temple at Ellora. Her reader moves with something of the excitement of the soldier who discovered that series of caves when out hunting, but the author's stance is that of the first sculptor as he paused on the volcanic outcrop to imagine his way down into the living rock. An artist's work has always been to chip away in a mineral darkness, but Mohanty brings to what might have turned an abstract project (the uncovering of a design fully formed in the head) a private tenderness as she discovers image after image of a love whose emblem is the sexless caress, of lovers leaning out into nothing, of strangers meeting and touching in a mausoleum or in a painted forest.'

I. Allan Sealy

'A book as vast as the world, as light as breath, as passionate as love, as humble as prayer. Sharmistha Mohanty has written an enchanting book, profound and delicate, a book to which I feel particularly close: life as a journey, to discover oneself and others; the journey as an immersion into a different time, into a present that widens out to embrace the world, in its various faces, colours, landscapes, destinies. A journey in which the self rediscovers the most authentic truth about itself, losing itself in the landscape and in others, becoming truly anonymous or concretely universal rather than vainly subjective, as the self always is when it loves, roams, when it watches the flow of a river, the shadow descending into the valleys, the ruins of the ancient cities and the garbage of modern ones. A lucid and relentless book, but a book of praise and love – for things, others, life.'

Claudio Magris

cntxt
book
one
SHARMISTHA
MOHANTY

cntxt

First published as a limited edition in 1995

Published by Context, an imprint of Westland Books, a division of
Nasadiya Technologies Private Limited, in 2023

No. 269/2B, First Floor, 'Irai Arul', Vimalraj Street, Nethaji Nagar,
Alapakkam Main Road, Maduravoyal, Chennai 600095

Westland, the Westland logo, Context and the Context logo are the
trademarks of Nasadiya Technologies Private Limited, or its affiliates.

ISBN: 9789357769488

10 9 8 7 6 5 4 3 2 1

Typeset by Jojy Philip, New Delhi
Printed at Parksons Graphics Pvt. Ltd

Contents

For my father, who imparted life to me. This giving of life was an act beyond the laws of biology, an act at once profound, subtle, ever-changing and manifold, with a beginning of course, but no end. Even now, many years after his death, my father continues to bring me life.

Ranesh Chandra Ghosh, 1921–1985

I hold out this book:

To James Alan McPherson, a teacher so complete that only with him did my writing grow and cease to matter at the same time

To Mani Kaul, who illuminated what was most ineffable, and changed more than the life of this book

To the warm, life affirming presence of U.R. Ananthamurthy for so many years

To the energetic and expansive Bob Shacochis, who has helped me, act and word, ever since the Iowa days

To Udayan Patel, not only in gratitude for mango trees and wide open spaces and time, but more in the joy of knowing that this book led me to him

And to Mummy and Baba, who gave me an entirely new world in which nothing was impossible.

Solitude

If you have lived, always, in these cities, and you go
away up to the mountains or down to a sea, you take a
long breath. I know how the sun and shadow move in
the mountains, how the sea never tires, nor the eye of
watching it. But I am here and I use my room like a cave or
a cell, sleeping, reading, eating. I chart the movement of
the sun in a small way. It falls here completely only in the
afternoons, almost with a cruel force and heat. I welcome
the moonrise. I take all the crumbs that the sky and wind
throw into my bare hands.

In the day the trees sway sometimes, but in this heat
they tend to be more still than ever. In the evening I get
reflected on the windowpanes. One's own face cannot be
looked at even for a moment, or it must be looked at for a
long, long time. I always choose the former. The mystery
of my features never reveals itself to me. Whoever sees
me sitting by the window, my face lit by the lamp, or
partly hidden in the new blue evening, bids me to action.
I don't understand. My limbs, in a manner of speaking,
are locked into place. I understand that people live, eat
together, make love, and visit each other. They travel,

they go on natural explorations. They teach, they study, they marry. I have done some of these things, not others. Why should I move? I feel little need to take my body and myself out of this room, this house, and out into the world.

The world is indeed intricate, fecund, full of births and deaths, beauty and violence. I watch a bee travelling on the windowpane. It is the colour of holud and its body has the most delicate orange lines on it. A fly near the lamp has a bright rust head, wings like glass and a smoky black body. Nothing in the world is a product of indifference.

The evening comes, emptying out of me even the small movements of heat and harsh light. I sit alone, I lie alone. There is only the inside landscape. It has its own laws, not that of the man-made world, not even that of nature. Perhaps I should not call it a landscape. It is more like something that flies over and away from the dead earth of circumstance and the narrative of birth to death.

I am alone here and I accept no metaphors, no teachers, no lovers. Nothing but a passing companion whose circumference might lightly touch mine.

Words

Beyond the borders of the mind, words awaken. They lose their certainty, they venture into life, not to define, but merely and simply, to live. They change their meanings, they contain experiences or the breaking of them. They are formed of incompleteness, of comings and goings, reaching and spilling over.

Breath

I breathe in, I breathe out. I look at the trees outside.
They bend to the breeze, then raise themselves up
again. I breathe in, I breathe out. I close my eyes. There
is a serenity in this breathing that comes from its utter
thoughtlessness. No other action is as unconscious, not
even the moving of an eyelid. When I breathe in, oxygen
and nitrogen enter inside me, substances breathed in by
all land animals and plants. Yet, when I breathe, I lose the
knowledge of this, I lose even the knowledge of breathing.
I take and I give back. This is the deepest of exchanges,
yet I cannot touch it with my bare hands. Only if I put
a solitary finger in the path of this breath, do I feel a
warmth, I feel a movement. The essence of breathing and
love are one.

'What Has Happened to Me?'

Tagore, in his great story, '*Nashtanir*', or Broken Nest, describes the relationship between a young woman and her brother-in-law, within the confines of a traditional Bengali family, early in this century. When her brother-in-law leaves for England, the woman is left alone with her pain.

'Charu was bewildered by all the movement within her, by her own unbearable pain. It was a torment without rest. She asked herself constantly, "Why? Why so much pain? What is Amal to me, that I should feel so much pain? What has happened to me? After so long, what is this that has happened to me?"'

I thought, at first, that this was an expression of a culture that had so repressed some emotions that people could no longer even find words to describe them, or give them meaning. These lines contain the essence of Tagore's story, but for a completely different reason. Neither here, nor anywhere else in the story, does Tagore mention the word love to describe Charu's emotions, or her husband's, or her brother-in-law's. I understand his deep restraint, and his final inability to use the word.

The Sari

The sari, as we know it now, was not worn in this ancient land. Epochs ago it was a piece of cloth tied around the waist and reaching the knees, as in the frescoes of Ajanta or the sculptures of old temples. Women wore nothing over their breasts. Slowly, the sari began to drape its way up. The breasts were covered, by a small piece of cloth. With the coming of Islam women began to wear a longer garment below the waist, it reached till the ankles. Above, the piece of cloth over the breasts grew into a full bodice, with arms and shoulders covered. A cloth, the dupatta, fell softly now, over the head. It did not take much time for the bodice to close the gap between it and the skirt, for the dupatta to grow longer till one side was tucked in to the skirt, the other end coming over the head, covering the bodice and reaching the waist. The lengthening of the dupatta was infinite. The sari finally emerged from a long dupatta, tucked into the skirt underneath at one end, going once around the body and then pulled all the way over the head at the other. Everything was covered now, the skirt, the bodice, the head. No skin showed, anywhere.

There was so much covering cloth that with the leftovers
women created pleats in front. The pleats flew a little as
they walked, on a summer evening full of released breeze.

Infinity

Once, I drove inland from the eastern coast of a far country. As I left behind the deep green hills of the east, I felt more of a stranger. The land turned a weak green and flattened overnight. There were no trees, no hills and mountains, not a single undulation, no flowers. No more buffers of nature, no more of what we all call beauty. Driving through, the expectation of these things began slowly to disappear, then, even the knowledge of them.

Wherever this may be, it is no place I have been to before. There is a calmness that I will not yet venture to call peace. This calmness is not an interval between two spaces and times, but rolling and continuous. It is defined best by its lack of sharpness. Otherwise I always live with things that are sharp, feelings and emotions twisting my body. They are like instruments—hammers, knives, razors and sticks—they impart movement, almost helplessly, to my hands. They are all gone now, these desires, images, these longings. They moved away so slowly, so silently, that I did not know the moment of their leaving. If need be, when they come back, I will not know how to ask them to leave again.

Somewhere

Wherever I may be now, only love and solitude remain. They take on each other's dimensions.

Flight

Something flies out of her to him before she can tell it to fly. Something lives inside her for him that works completely unbidden, that is free even from her deepest desires.

Bird

Last spring I lived in a large house on the hills. There was a dog, a fearful cat, three docile goats, and of course, the birds. One evening, returning from my walk among the winding hill roads, I saw the dog charging at something in one corner of the porch. In the dim yellow light I saw a little bird, with a small brown and white flecked body, crouched near a door. It was wounded perhaps, and couldn't fly, only raise itself a few inches with a great fluttering of wings. Each time the dog ran towards it the bird managed to rise a little and then fell back down.

To save it from the dog I captured it in a white bowl put upside down on a plate and took it in. I took the bowl off and put a colander in its place so it could breathe. I put in some grains of rice through the holes. The bird didn't eat, it fluttered, it fretted inside, and all one could see through the holes was this desperate movement. Only once or twice it sat quiet and I saw its diminutive, clear eyes and its perfect body.

There was a valley falling deep below the house, a valley with pine trees and terraced farms. I thought I could free the bird at the edge of the house, from where it could fall, not a very great height, onto a bush in the valley, and be safe from dogs. I took it out underneath the colander. It was cold outside and there were pieces of tattered clouds floating in the darkness of the valley. There was a lowered terrace at the edge of the house. I went to the edge of this terrace, leant over far into the night and lifted the colander. The bird flew out as if it had known this precise moment when it would be called upon to fly. It flew away without a struggle as if this unexpected captivity had wiped away its wounds, wherever they were, and after a short, short burst of flight from the colander it hung suspended over the dark valley for one solitary moment and it moved its wings, slowly, in great silence. Then it gave a small, delicate cry as small birds often will but the cry was drawn out, elongated, and with it the bird cleaved the darkness and flew away.

My Mother

I always think of my mother's pain, when I'm not near her. I see her like a black and white photograph, a white widow in a dark, empty, falling house. Then, I seem to touch her pain, and when I go to her next, I am completely prepared to cradle her pain in my arms. When I meet her and embrace her, she keeps her arms hanging stiffly at the sides. She asks me how I am.

'Well,' I tell her.

'But what about my pain?' she asks, and throws all her despair into my arms. At this close distance her pain loses its metaphorical, imaginary quality. Her despair is mean, small and ugly, it spills over my arms, into the room, and out onto the street. My mother is so real that I can never pass right through her.

Lines

The skin under his eyes is soft, with three soft little
ridges beneath each eye. Most of the day he smiles, talks,
explains, his hands fly. These ridges are hidden then. They
are shadowed over by the brightness of his eyes. Only
when the afternoon is hot and he lays down his agile
body, or at night, late, by lamplight, the ridges appear. She
touches them, carefully, with the tip of her forefinger. The
lines etched firmly into her finger, skin lines, float over
the ridges of the eyes.

Mouths, noses and eyes are completely formed on a
person's face. Lines are more vulnerable. The face is not
always aware of its own lines. Even the watcher, who
knows that those lines exist, is surprised every time they
appear. She does not know when he will smile. When
he does, she becomes, truly, a watcher, and she sees the
lines around his mouth being pushed by the energy of
the smile into slim furrows, the one on the left so much
deeper than the one on the right.

Dust

Dust settles on everything. A mute, winter dust, unspectacular, unlike the violent duststorms of summer's rage. There is this dust, unspeaking, and for the first time in the year, light, that is clear, golden and recognisable as light. After the summer, when light was a dead continuum of heat and haze, now when I step out I have to pause, for a moment, before its perfect clarity.

Under the dust, the world seems old. Even the trees, green in this tropical winter, have dust on the leaves. People are dying in the Congo, they are starving in nearby villages, they are going to the movies in large, tired cities running on their last breath for a decade, they are flying the sky and waiting in transit lounges where voices are saying, 'Attention, please. The flight is now ready for departure. Passengers are requested to …' What will be new? Surely, not that which is not old.

There are weak wisps of air that sometimes disturb the dust, shifting it a little, making a clearing for a forefinger. These wisps cannot be touched of course, because they are air, yet they are not breath for they cannot sustain life.

Death

The front door is open like a flung out arm and no one stands there. At the top of the stairs are the people, not scattered at random, but pressed flat against the walls in the long hallways. There is a cousin, not seen in years, who now with head bent and brimming eyes comes close, too close, and touches me gently on one arm. The kitchen is deserted. The coal fire has not even been lit and the milk lies uncovered in the kansa bowl, waiting to be boiled. There are flowers, but only white. And no one, no one will raise their face and meet my eyes.

I reach my father's room.

The soul is not this, not that. It is unseizable, for it cannot be seized; indestructible, for it cannot be destroyed, unattached, for it cannot attach itself; is unbound, does not tremble, is not injured …

I double over and reach the ground in my bending and I know that pain is not pain till it is of the body, that never before have I felt pain, and that words are made up by the mind, and I can never speak again but only make these endless rising and falling sounds with my mouth, azaan from the minaret sounds circling in the blue sky, animal sounds, coming from landscapes the mind will never know.

After these sounds, there is silence.

This is a silence that marks the end of hope, the end of the heart's movement, the heart's flight, for what is there left to fly towards, and most of all it is the silence of the end, the fact of an end, this is the end, this forcing of the heart to be still forever when it longs for nothing but to move.

Understanding

'My love,' they all say, every one of them.
'My love,' holding my face in their hands.
'My love,' while I arch under them.
'My love,' as they look at me, sitting in silence.
Will I ever understand what they mean?

Darkness

In this darkness there is no seeing, open the eyes as wide
as you will. This darkness like never before will not allow
itself to be lifted, even in one corner of its veil. It will no
longer allow her to speak, for one moment to emerge
as herself to ask of someone she loves. She looks at her
hands, the nails bitten, the skin rough and dark. There is
nothing left for her to do but to study her own body. Her
hands are very much like her father's. But her wrists are
narrow and fragile. Her feet are rough and brown like her
hands. All her extremities seem unnecessarily hardened.
Her arms are smooth though and her legs. She turns her
hands around so she can see the backs and the palms. She
looks carefully at the top of her feet. They are not symbols
of anything, they are hands and feet.

She stays with this darkness because she is not capable
any longer of shedding anything. It stays with her. No
distractions, no pleasures, not a single pinhole of light.
For the first time, she and her darkness are one.

Nothing

When I was a child I used to close my eyes and imagine 'nothing'. No me, no room, no world, no stars, nothing at all. I squeezed shut my eyes and sat hunched in darkness. My mind, of course, would not let me discover 'nothing', there were scraps of memories and thoughts falling into this black night. But most of all I would get tired of squeezing my eyes shut so tight. I would slacken and in would come a shred of lamplight from another room, the mind would rush towards it like a heart towards whatever it understands of love. Nothing would quickly become everything. The sound of voices, the furniture, the porcelain container of a father's love. The world would rush back, object by familiar object.

The House

My grandmother was sitting in the kitchen one day, stirring the yellow dal in a large earthen pot on the coal fire, when a piece of the ceiling fell on her back. My grandmother, a soft, large, plump woman, sat down on the floor without a single cry of pain. It took six months for her back to heal. For a few days the rafters showed if we looked up inside the kitchen but then the fixing men came and put things back in their place.

In this house, built by my grandfather, my mother still lives in her widowhood. Alone, her whole day is spent in curing the rotted wooden beams, looking after the spreading patches of damp on the ceiling, fixing panes of glass that the wind has broken loose from the windows. In the monsoons, when we sit down to dinner, the drops falling from the ceiling onto the table make a discrete, distinguishable sound against the backdrop of sheets of falling rain outside. My mother eats in silence, listening to the drops, counting the days when she will have to move to a new house without her life and her memories. The new house, she says, will contain only her death.

At breakfast the next day, a huge patch of plaster falls from above. I hold it in my hand, and it is nothing more than plaster, dry and white. 'Leave it,' says my mother. 'The house is falling.'

Walking

I walk, forever, in this house. In my sari, with the pleats crumpled, and my black hair knotted loosely at my neck, always at the point where it will soon slip onto my back. I have already cut my hair but I will always wear my hair long, just as I will always walk in this house though I have long ago abandoned it. My mother walks here too, endlessly, like myself, in a white sari, always in the opposite direction so I can see her face to face, the whiteness of her skin, sari and hair.

There are windows and doors, windows and doors, doors and windows, on the edges of this house, always open and without curtains. This house lets in everything, the diaphanous morning, voices and laughter, the music of the bearded ektara player who has played on this very street for one hundred years.

We stay away from the sun as we walk, it is too much for us both. The day passes, as we wait in the shadows, finally arriving at its twilight. Only at such an unreal time do my mother and I have the courage to be real. We gather up our saris, pressing down the pleats into place, hooking up our blouses, knotting our hair at the nape with our hands. My mother's sari is no longer so white.

We look through the open doors and windows. It is only in this twilight that the horizon makes any sense at all. It is now that everything meets, light and darkness, sky and land, fulfilling for a time our whole day's yearning for unities. My mother waits for these moments as one waits for grace, never really knowing the time of their arrival.

Flower

A root and stem and leaves and bud taken to their fullest possibility will form a flower. Nothing less.

The Fall

It was the most languorous of falls. She spiralled, she floated on the air, in the rain filled darkness, watching a smothered horizon, moving towards it, knowing that it will always keep moving further away. She fell past windows, little unflickering lamps or squares of dark behind which people slept in warm beds and kissed their children fresh with the smell of milk. From the outside the windows felt so natural that she felt for them the compassion that one has for the most delicately ubiquitous things, like a blade of grass. Faces watched her from some windows, a pane of glass flew open somewhere in the rain. The rain was in her eyes, the rain was collecting at the nape of her neck, in droplets at the tips of her fingers. She could see as she fell the sombre trees, and the poignance that streetlamps have only in the rain. But they were no longer tree and light, nothing she had known before, because nothing she had known before had ever risen up like this to meet her.

Undefinable

In my solitude.

In my solitude I am neither man nor woman. If I were in loneliness I would be sharp and angular as one of the two. Sifting things through a sieve, choosing a few elements, rejecting others. In solitude I pass beyond choices. The privilege of solitude is to be undefinable, very precisely human.

Memory

On evenings like this one, when the breeze is full of a fading winter and an approaching summer, I do not dwell for too long on my dead father with his quiet eyes like mine. His coming close to me and holding my face in his hands would mean my own death. My survival is at stake.

When a memory comes like one white fluffed feather, I watch it float by at a distance.

I am twelve and love to place my head between my father's neck and shoulders and smell his fatherly smell, so utterly human yet so inseparable from nature, that in that hollow I feel him and smell him like a tree bark in sunlight. I want to lie there with my head in that place, touching the soft roughness of the bark with my face half in sun and half in shade. I swing my legs from the height of his lap.

When I am twelve a drop of blood falls from between my legs. A new silence comes from the power of this blood. It is too much for me, this silence I have never known before. I'm wounded, I'm dying. I tell my father, running to him in my white slip that just reaches my thighs, with its straps falling away from my shoulder, I tell my father, listen, do you know I'm dying? Come, I say, and take him by the hand to the drops of blood on the floor. He says, 'It's—' and puts his hand on the top of my head.

Afternoon

On a winter afternoon, the world is dusty and old. What is there left to do? A young boy walks by, through rectangles of clear winter light, with a donkey. The animal has a sadness beyond vulnerability, and the boy an openness, to the road and the winter sky. On the back of the donkey are piled clay pots that gently strike against one another as the donkey moves. The boy looks at the houses he passes by, one hand on the donkey's reins, the other deep in the pocket of his trousers.

The left hand holds the city in his pocket, the right hand, the reins to the countryside. That is the mind speaking, jealous of the watcher watching, entering, this tender young boy, this sad animal, dust coloured. On a winter afternoon the mind turns on itself, the self folds and wrinkles. There is nothing left for the mind and the self to do but separate further and further like two paths in the wilderness. There is nothing left till, like those two paths, they suddenly join or cross each other, behind a corner, at right angles. Poised on the edge of a leaf, the afternoon waits, for flight.

Hands

Suddenly he holds her small breasts, taking her unawares with his long, slender hands. His hands are large, her feet are small, her feet are precisely the size of his hands.

Birth

No, not a child, nothing formed as perfectly as a child.
Nothing yet with a life of its own.

Tornado

On the day the tornado came, my grandfather saw a buffalo fly through the air. Not gently, its large body resting on the flow of the breeze, but sudden and swift, like an afternoon sleep's oversized dream. It was so close when it went by that he could have reached out and touched its frightened face.

My grandfather, in a long white shirt and dhoti, was on his way back from a walk. As the breeze intensified, his dhoti swirled around his legs. The black umbrella he also used as a cane was sucked away from his hand. There were red and yellow flowers, broken from their stalks and flying over the fields. The flower filled wind threw my grandfather against a banyan tree. On all fours, little by little, he made his way home. On the way he saw a cow on a peepul tree and small silver fish on bushes. He passed the neighbourhood pond from which this wind had drained all the water and hurled it on the land. The pond was empty now, a large bowl of weeds and silt.

All night, the wind. All night the sound of falling trees, breaking branches, dancing twigs, flowers hurled against one another. In the lantern light, full of shadows, my grandfather sat silently. No other sound, no other action, except the wind's had any meaning. So he made only the most necessary of movements—stretching a leg, waving away a moth, leaning his head against a wall. His mind hovered in a region beyond fear, beyond wonder. The wind had entered him and had begun to move him inside, gently but powerfully, a slow wave forming from the sea of his blood.

A window flew open towards midnight, and my grandfather, looking out, saw a large crystal chandelier floating through the dark, all its swaying pieces tinkling loudly against each other. The zamindar, my great grandfather, was slowly losing his riches to the wind. The chandelier was like a star flung down from the sky, stark against the tornado night blackness. The world had changed, thought my grandfather. In the relentless wind, things had been cut loose from their moorings. The chandelier was a low hanging star, the buffalo a bird, the pond a crater, the land a lake.

The wind transformed things, gave them new names. And not only new names. It gave them new possibilities.

The chandelier knew how it felt to be a star, and the silver fish what it was to be a bird on a green smelling bush. My grandfather opened his eyes in the tornado to a new vision of the world. He saw that only things loosened from their moorings became truly real, like a ship throwing off anchor to set sail.

When my grandfather came to the city, he carried the wind with him. In the big city house, he was the one who breathed most easily, sitting on the bed with his back straight, his hands on his knees, silent. There were large balconies in the house but still too many walls, and the wind entered here only in small wisps, like a child's excited breath. Once, only once, it knocked over a glass.

Eating

My grandfather, when he ate, sat before a large kansa plate ringed by kansa bowls containing rice and fish and vegetables. He ate slowly, finishing the food in each bowl before moving on to the next. 'You must chew each mouthful carefully,' he would tell me. 'Never gulp anything down. Take your time, chew carefully, then swallow.' I watched my grandfather eat. At the end he would drink water from a large bell metal glass. He would drink it all, the whole glass, he never left a drop behind.

Food

In the falling house my mother lives out her days. She cooks, endlessly, over the ancient coal oven once used by my grandmother. When the fire dies down, she fans it, and when it dies down beyond revival, she moves reluctantly to the new, white electric stove and oven. When she moves here, the earth colours of mud, coal and orange fire linger in the eyes of anyone who is visiting her.

She cooks with an intense concentration that brings out the sweat on her forehead where a white wisp of hair hangs. There is moisture on her upper lip, her nose and her armpits. It is May, and the black ants of summer's cruelty, of summer's rage, crawl slowly in the balcony sun.

Everything is fried in mustard oil. My mother cooks with subtlety and delicacy but the oil is her road to excess. Its heavy, lingering smell spreads over the house and brings down small flakes of plaster from overhead. She throws flour, vegetables and seeds into this oil. The remnants get fried to crisps and settle at the bottom.

She cooks vegetables, fried fish, she cooks milky rasamalais. Everything is perfect, even when she is hurried, even when there is no one to eat what she cooks. My mother cooks whole meals even when she is not expecting guests, though, of course, someone may perhaps come.

The two servants help her as she cooks. They prepare things. They boil potatoes, thicken milk, grind the spices to a paste and transfer it neatly to separate bowls ready for my mother to use. The man servant, as old as my mother, is emaciated from lack of money, two wives and eight children. He brings to cooking only something that resembles energy, he can do no more. My mother shows something resembling acceptance, though, as she watches the vegetables fry, her lips tighten. 'I need some more milk for the children,' he says. 'Take it,' says my mother, wiping the sweat on her forehead with her left arm.

My mother's white sari has spots of holud and oil on it, just where her thin breasts are covered by her blouse. She loves these spots and will not look at them if you point them out to her. Instead she will show you her arms and hands, which have blisters and burns from so much

     SHARMISTHA MOHANTY

frying, from oil that has jumped back from the pan to her skin. 'I don't even care about these,' she will say.

The woman servant is older than my mother. She stands next to my mother, also in a white sari, but a white that is far less bright and clear. She always does what she wants and hits her chest with her fists when contradicted. She talks to herself as she walks down the long, dark hallways. My mother accepts by pressing her lips together. This time they twitch a little at the ends. The only time the woman servant is quiet is when evening comes. She has been a widow since she was fourteen and came to the house to work for my grandparents. In the evening she always sits on the balcony and looks up at the moon growing full or lean in the sky.

'Parul … Parul,' my mother calls her. 'The milk is going to boil over.' Parul doesn't get up. After a while my mother comes looking for her, through all the rooms and finally out onto the balcony. She discovers Parul looking at the sky. She says, 'I've been looking for you everywhere,' and leaves. My mother would never dare to look at the moon.

Astral Dreams

The dreams, though there is conversation and argument, are silent in the way it is only possible for dreams to be. She dreams of airplanes. She cannot board. Her ticket has expired, her luggage is lost. There is always a reason that cannot be suspended and she is always alone with the man at the counter.

Change is slow, even in the pattern of dreams. Eventually she dreams she is on a very large airplane, a person in every seat. They fly through darkness but outside it is not the sky that she looks up at from earth, it is the blackness of void, of something beyond the known universe. Since it is not the sky, neither she nor the others can know where they are going.

Change is like a gift, even in the pattern of dreams. Only when she has forgotten about the airplanes do her dreams turn truly astral. She is in the sky, herself, no airplanes, no vehicles at all. Before her a sphere like the moon hangs brightly.

As she looks at it the sphere rends apart in two places to show her, through these new clearings, all that is possible for her to see. She sees comets with blazing orange trails, a far planet. She knows that the sphere is revealing itself for her. She knows this as a moment of beginning. She sees the light of many stars.

The sky has come down to stay with her.

Destiny

He kissed her breasts as if making up for lost time, as if he was in a hurry, though time had neither been lost nor was in the course of being taken away. She watched, in the gaps between when his love closed her eyes and she saw nothing. She watched the curve of a breast, his lips on it, his eyes closed, his mouth on the dark brown nipple. She held his head with its thick hair between her hands as if he were a bird with the skull of a man.

At the end of every lovemaking her breasts returned to their own serenity, undestroyed. Memories of mouths hovered over them and fell away. Her destiny was contained in her breasts.

Tree

The top of the mango tree is becoming brown in the April heat, brown and withered and limp. The rest of the tree is full and green. Its long, slender leaves come in clusters, hanging downwards. They are so plentiful that only by looking closely at them in the sharp sun can anything else be seen. In a small, shadowed space between the leaves a sparrow sits, swivelling its small head. The sparrow is light brown like the top of the tree. From the dense growth further in a golden oriole suddenly flies out, shaking the leaves and branches.

When a great gust of wind blows, small bits of green shake that are not leaves. They are diminutive new mangoes, hanging from the tree by their thin green stems, small enough to fit in the centre of the palm and close the fingers over, deep green, and with the sour-fresh smell that is hot summer. Later, the sun will ripen them as it does no other fruit. Outside, the skin will lose its deep green uniformity. Inside, the sun will give this fruit its own colours in the fullness of its spectrum—to each fruit a different hue—it will give the quiet gold of its rising, the deep orange of its going down or the almost colourless yellow of its noontime.

Underneath the voluminous shade of this mango tree a man sits, protected from the April sun. He rests his head on his knees, a strong, lean man with a thick moustache. A little girl passes by, perhaps no more than ten years old, a girl with her white dupatta dirty and torn. Her hair is as brown and dusty as the road she walks on, her feet bare. She stops under the fullness of the mango tree. She sees the small, unripe mangoes and asks the man to pick one for her. The man stands up and reaches high. He pulls a branch towards him and plucks one small mango. The girl takes the mango in her hand and smiles. The pulled branch swings back upwards, repositioning itself, and stays in gentle motion for a few moments.

There is now a love in me greater than the love I have always been able to give.

Worship

The sky during this time of year is supposed to be a clear, cloudless blue, but there is a canopy of brown cloth over the moving circle, so the sky cannot be seen. This is the last day of Durga Puja, and my mother walks in a circle with fifteen other women, around the seven foot clay image of Durga standing on a large platform. The women move slowly, barefoot, wearing white saris with red borders. They have large dots of sindoor on their forehead, larger than usual, and they hold brass plates in their hands. On the plates there are offerings to Durga. There are little pots of sindoor, sweets, leaves of fresh green paan, small piles of rice inside the husk and some blades of new grass.

The circle is only for married women. My mother loves being a part of circles anywhere but she never really fits in. Here, she is the most beautiful of all the women. She walks around the deity, her face eager with worship. The other women, less beautiful, but more real, walk more casually.

In this stance of worship, their saris covering their heads, there are traces of the night when they twisted their bodies in bed, traces of their days, hard and linear and endless. But in my mother there is only the face raised upwards and no hint of her days and nights.

There are small, shaky wooden stairs which the women climb one by one to reach the face of Durga, with its large dark eyes and faint smile. From the brass plate they hold out a sweet at the clay mouth, caress the cheeks with a leaf of paan, they put sindoor in the parting of her hair and the rice grains and grass they scatter over her head. When my mother's turn comes she walks up the shaking stairs with trembling legs. She steadies herself before the deity. Then she begins. I cannot see her face. Only her back is towards me with her freshly washed hair falling till her waist. She stays in front of Durga's face for so long that below her the circle becomes restless.

She cannot stop the paan leaf caress. She goes on and on but her arms do not seem to tire. The sindoor she puts on the parting of Durga's clay black hair, then smears it on the flesh coloured clay cheeks, arms and neck. She cannot stop. Her shoulders gather together. She feeds Durga the white sweets till the red painted clay mouth is covered with this soft white substance.

Bodies

The skin was wrinkled, rough and loose, yet their smiles were firm and completely painless. My grandparents had faces I have never seen again, anywhere. Their silences, when they sat alone inside, or in the balcony sun, were strong and unflickering. Their faces were full of life lived, life seen, with perhaps a few traces of wistfulness.

My grandmother wore six golden bangles, three on her right arm, three on her left. 'These I will leave to you,' she would tell me, smiling and touching me under the chin. 'They're my most precious possessions. I've worn them all my life.' When my grandmother took off her sari she revealed a white cotton chemise that reached till her knees. Her body was plump, the arms enormous and wide, her breasts large and hanging down almost till her swollen stomach. Her thighs were heavy and thick and at the very end of her body, on her two feet, the skin had scaled off to reveal an underlayer of light red tissue that meant relentless eczema. When she walked, she swayed a bit, from side to side. Her enormity included everything, her children, her house, her husband, and all the world outside.

My parents had faces full of grief and restlessness and desire. My father's body was stout and strong, yet he suffered all his life from diseases. They were diseases he always harboured inside, that grew in his depths till he had to be opened and the diseases cut out. Ulcers, gallbladder stones, cysts, boils. In the end, when my father became most weak and his walk slowed down, he declared, 'Now I've got cancer.' The doctor, the next day, confirmed this verdict. My father's black hair fell, in clumps, all over the house. His dark body began to resemble the colour of burnt earth. He couldn't eat the food he so loved, the fish in mustard paste, the sweets in syrup. 'I'm dying', he told us. When they brought his body home, covered with flowers, his cheeks were concave and cold. The lips were stretched open in pain.

My mother has a body that is primarily pain's own receptacle. Her intestines are too long and coiled up, so it is painful for her, every day, to empty her bowels. She eats, only to live somehow, eats too little, and her stomach is full of the most bilious juices that corrode her insides. There is a slow cataract spreading over her eyes.

Sometimes when she is too ill to move, I help her to take off her clothes. Thin breasts hang on her chest. They have shrunk from the fullness I remember to small pieces of wrinkled skin. From the breasts to her stomach there are a series of horizontal wrinkles. The stomach itself hangs loose over the beginning of emaciated thighs. She is white all over, from the hair on her head, to the skin all over her body. Only the triangle between her thighs is still covered with black hair that seems anachronistic in all this faded paleness. My mother falls ill all the time, but she outlives everything. Outside, her body is slow, the flesh is crumpled and hanging loose. But, says my mother, in great pain, 'Inside, I have a pair of lungs and a heart of steel. I live and live and live.'

Nameless

The thing she cannot touch is what comes from him, whether it is she who takes or he who gives. She watches it come through a sky between them, flying high in it, she sees it arc and spiral and drop into the deep, deep well. It is a stone, she thinks, it has cleaved the water's depth and sunk right to the bottom where it will hold still for centuries and get covered with the softest moss.

But after the first stillness the thing begins to tremble. It is a pool of light on the water's surface. It pushes up and half closes her tender eyelids.

It leaves even trembling behind. It swims. A fish.

Asking

In these dead river days, full of the taste of ashes and dust, when everything in the air settles, something must also rise. Not like a woman in her lover's arms, there has been too much of that.

In the early morning her sleep is covered over by dust. She opens her eyes. The world is submerged by ashes, more settling from the death of unknown fires near her. In a square of sunlight she sits up straight as something comes twisting and rolling from inside. She brings her hands together in prayer for the very first time, and waits. Only then she sees that she doesn't know what to ask for.

The days are becoming longer, the sun setting later and later, the birds flying back even later than the sun, the dust collecting even after sundown.

Landscapes

In the evening heat of a peaking summer, among people going home from wilted days, came the fulfillment of a love. He stood behind her, so much taller, looking down at the top of her head, saying, 'You, you'll be my wife.' Her head, that he looked down at and softly kissed, while they waited to cross the evening street, held a heavy knot at the nape of the neck, made carelessly out of her waist length hair. On the street with people returning home and the birds of twilight flying above, when she knew for certain she would be his wife, the kiss spread all through the thick black streams of hair and came together again to form the knot, and its weight made her head tilt downward with love, so that she could no longer see the birds, and she was aware of a new life about to begin.

What did it mean for a life to be new?

Then one day she was in a vast land of ice and snow, flat land, where the horizon only kept moving further away, leaving more space for her loneliness. In the dark of night she travelled on the even darker roads of these flat lands, past fields of snow on either side. Moving onwards, the car came upon a layer of thin ice on the road. The wheels lost their grip and the car began to turn in slow, hesitant circles on the ice. Once, and she saw how dark the sky was, without a moon. Twice, and she saw how dark the sky was again, no stars. Three times the car circled, and the third time she took her eyes away from the sky. The car stopped, she sat in silence. Her father was dead.

Why had she come to this country so far away, away from her father when he died? Why was she here now, even after his death was done?

Once again, in another land—this world full of trees and birds and rocks and stones never ends. In the long dusks, the long, long dusks of the northern latitudes, the sky darkens slowly, to a deep blue that twists the heart. The green woods become dark as she walks along a dirt road, passing streams that fall over rocks and boulders. In a crevice between two rocks something shines as bright and still as a diamond. She watches for a few moments and the diamond dislodges itself. It is a firefly preparing to go forth into the evening.

Far above the firefly the sky slowly deepens to the edge
of darkness, but still blue and still giving enough light
to see by. The sky holds itself there for a long time. The
sky holds and sounds gather around her, a lone bird in
flight, water over rock. Above and beyond this, there
are the cries of children playing, calling each other, far
away, perhaps even beyond the next hill. Their calls are
drawn out, discrete, elongated, spreading slowly in the air
around them, and suddenly three horses gallop towards
her, gallop out of that twilight blue, just before the
completeness of dark night. They stop in front of her with
their dark manes and warm breath.

Why is the one she loves so far away?

 SHARMISTHA MOHANTY

Wedding

I know how my mother and father were at their wedding,
I know without being told. I've been watching weddings
ever since I was a child and longed to be a bride myself. On
the third day, when the wedding rituals had ended, the
groom took the bride away to his home. This was always in
the afternoon, when the light was harsh and unwelcome.
Always, the bride and groom, before leaving, sat beside
each other on the ground to receive the blessings of
the elders. As aunts and uncles and older cousins came
one after another, placing the new grass and paddy on
the heads of the married couple, and as the bride, more
humbly than the groom, touched the elders' feet, the
sorrow of departure gathered inside her. Sometimes, in
between the touching of feet with jewelled hands, she
looked around at the bouquets of dying flowers, trying to
imagine a new home, but knowing deep down that new
homes can never be imagined.

The bride began to cry, softly at first, and then, when it
was her parents' turn to bless, she cried loud, bitter tears,
while the father restrained himself, his eyes moist and

the mother turned away, weeping into the aanchal of her
sari which she had brought to her face. Through all this
the groom sat with an air of patience, waiting to leave, a
little weary of this brimming sorrow he could not really
understand. At last they would leave, and from inside the
car the bride stretched out her hands to clasp the palms
and arms and wrists of all those she had loved in her
former life.

When my parents sat being blessed by the elders, my
mother's only brother fell on the floor crying, and my
widower grandfather, in between his restrained tears,
asked, 'Can't you take her away tomorrow instead of today?'

'No,' said my father's family. 'It is inauspicious to leave her
here after the wedding is complete.'

My father, gentler, so much gentler than other men,
hesitated for a while, sitting there on the ground beside
his new wife. But in the end, wasn't he a man and didn't
he have to take his bride home? He stood up slowly and
adjusted his dhoti and kurta, he took one step forward. My
mother, the aanchal of her sari tied in a knot with the end
of her husband's kurta, followed him out of her parents'
home.

Banana Tree

When she was brought through the door women gathered around in celebration, blowing conch shells with all their breath, their throats swelling, their eyes closed. The banana tree bride was the goddess Lakshmi and she was welcomed in with an affectionate reverence. As she was carried up the stairs, the women bent a little forward and down before her, for how could wealth and prosperity ever be taken for granted? Every year she came to our home, a week after Durga Pujas, and she was brought to an inner room and placed carefully by the window where she could still feel a remnant of the breeze she had known outside.

In fact, the banana tree bride was part of a banana tree, standing on a long green trunk which was so pliant that it bent to one side. The trunk then flowed into a slender, green branch, at the end of which hung the banana leaf, with a broad rib in the middle and two soft pieces of square green hanging down on either side, each with its own thin ribs running through it from top to bottom.

My mother bathed and dressed the bride. She put on Lakshmi her own wedding sari, a fabric of dark red with golden mangoes spread all over. The sari wound its way around the trunk, covering it completely, the aanchal went over the neck formed by the branch, and was pulled over the part where the leaf began. It was the leaf which was the face of the banana tree bride and it hung downward without any divine gravity but full of a shy tenderness, as if she were a real Bengali bride from centuries ago who would take a long time to show us her face.

It was to her that all the offerings were made, miniature temples and chariots of white sugar, grains of rice, fruits, and the coconut sweets that my grandmother had spent all day making. After the puja was over and we had all touched the elders' feet, we were given the prasad on small squares of banana leaf. As a child I cried and said, 'You've torn off Lakshmi's face.'

'Lakshmi has many faces,' said my grandmother, putting a wrinkled palm under my chin. 'Now eat.'

Long ago, someone walking with mud coloured feet like mine in the riverine lands of my grandfather's Bengal, someone with no knowledge of cities, had picked up a banana tree, put it on his shoulders so the broad leaves brushed his face, and brought it home to worship. It is the earth that throws up the truest metaphors.

Airplane

Inside an airplane, moving straight to another point in this endless world, people fall asleep on others' shoulders and throughout the night dream their astral dreams. They wake confused in the morning, not happy at having rested on unknown flesh and bone. They straighten their sleep creased faces and become distant again.

On earth, the mango tree is going through its eternal changes. The sun is making the tree dark green, hard for the eye to penetrate. When the clouds come, they lighten the tree's colour, and the tree turns generous, offering each of its infinite details. Every leaf can be seen clearly under the gentle clouds, with the one broad rib through the middle, the small ribs striking out on either side, and the random curves of the leaf edges. Far inside the branches there are two yellow leaves, close to a fall.

So many miles flown in the quiet air and morning passes, evening comes again, somewhere over fields and cities and rivers. On earth perhaps there is a storm lashing the windowpanes, there is the call of a koel just before dawn. There are faces that grow more understood with time, tales that are revealed, griefs that begin finally to understand each other.

When there is nowhere to leave for, it is the heart that gets unmoored, spreading through the body like a light, hovering with hope at the surface of the skin. People become eyes that slowly fill, faces to be touched lightly with the back of the hand, hands to be raised to the lips, necks and hunched shoulders and backs hiding the sorrow that stands before the face. All of this while the moving, spreading heart pushes away its own torments.

The rain that falls past the airplane is without body, soundless, uncommitted. Near the mango tree, it is a monsoon day, brimming with rhythm and movement. The clouds pass overhead, light ebbs, the rain falls, water streams and flows on the asphalt, trees bend to gusts of wind, birds fly to their shelters, children cover their heads with fronds of palm and walk barefoot through the falling water.

In the dark night, the airplane circles a snowstorm sky.

West

In a far city, in the bars filled with smoke, sharp with lust and drunkenness, behind laughing people with glasses at the mouth, there are old men with faces the colour of dark potato skins. Faces that were diggers of brown earth, old brown faces with the skin blown out below the eyes, quiet faces, watching everything. Their sad lake eyes bear the quiet indifference of those who have seen too much pain to ever be taken by surprise.

A woman comes and stands under a pool of light, large and heavy breasted, her body full of a thousand nights of deep lovemaking. She begins to sing a song that emerges from the fullness of her body with a gift and a grace that turn despair into melody. Only the song has the power to make the old men smile with their broad, bitten lips, and it adds the light of dusk to their sad lake eyes.

In the underground a wind blows, travelling in and out through the tunnels after the trains have left. It catches the ends of paisley scarves and the ties of men going to offices. It lifts the coats of elegant women, a cold wind, an insidious wind, an insistent wind. People turn their backs on it, firmly. There is so little time and life is yet to be lived.

Women of the east in the western hemisphere stand behind shop counters, their heads always covered. In the paleness of the face, a diamond nose pin shines like a remnant of dead longings. Their husbands watch over the shop, over them. The cash registers are grey, the bills are all neatly arranged. The pale coloured burkhas they wear cover the whole body save the face with enormous eyes and the fabric chafes their skins even in this gentle summer heat of the west.

The ripe golden fruits of another land sometimes have the taste of metal.

Pain

I return home from the burning ghats and stop at the doorstep. I bite on a neem leaf, touch a piece of iron with my hands, wash my feet and hold my palms over a pan with golden fire in it. I rub my warm hands in one clean sweep over my head and cross the threshold.

Inside, my mother is becoming a widow.

She takes off the iron bangle covered with gold that she has worn on her left arm ever since her wedding day and places it neatly on her dresser. She must now remove the unblemished white conch-shell bangles, also from the day she was married. As is the way in these parts, she breaks these bangles by hitting her arms against the wall. Uneven white pieces fall to the ground. My mother moves methodically to the mirror. She takes the end of her sari, wipes off the red dot on her forehead, then smoothly takes away the sindoor in the parting of her hair. Finally, she takes off the dark green sari she is wearing and puts on her sari of new widow white. The fabric rustles as she adjusts the aanchal and bends to smoothen the pleats. She looks at me then with a question in her eyes, as if to ask, 'Anything else? Is my widowhood complete?'

I am a grown woman now, no longer her child only, I have made love and travelled and explored and been bound in the fetters of grief more than once. Now, with my father's body freshly burnt I am older than ever.

With my sight getting sharper by the moment I see beyond the new widowhood, the beautiful woman who has shed all her colours of gold and red and green, and my sight rests on that constant involuntary twitch of her delicate lips and her lovely vacant eyes.

My mother, who follows rituals so exactly, and prays four times a day and decorates her puja room with such intensity and cooks to please all who have ever known her, is someone who has never experienced that movement that begins in the chest, tight as a pain, and travels upwards, expanding, and continues on the face in a flutter of the eyelid, in a slow, small turn that brings a face so close to another that one is silenced by the pores of the other's skin and the dark shadow thrown by an eye. In my mother's world, gestures hang in the air cut from their sources, a loosened smile, a gliding head bowed in prayer. Nothing has anchor and my mother, locked in her prison of bones, looks and looks for a reason for the flesh to survive but she finds nothing, for what reason can there ever be?

My gift of sight does not stop here. As my heart begins to twist and turn, away from my mother, it stops in its turning and holds still. It is the absolute and uncompassionate stillness of harsh summer, and all judgment, all accusations are stripped away from my body like scorched leaves. In my mother, standing before me, I face myself, I face what stops the world. It is not hate that is the opposite of love, it is not-love, and my mother is brimming with it. What emptiness this not-love is, what barrenness, what parched earth waiting eternally for the rains and I think of sages with beautiful faces and watching eyes, as tender and full of love and as dead as my father. My sight meets its horizon, darkness falls. Outside, people wait to mourn with the new widow. Inside, my mother is losing her widowhood, becoming nameless, amorphous, and it is on the white, colourless shoulders of the world, like a hardened ridge on the earth's crust, that I lay my frightened face.

Cremation

I hold three long wooden sticks, flaming at the end. Three
times I circle the body. Along with me moves a circle of
men, uncles, friends, cousins, moving behind me as I
move, cushioning me from what, protecting me, from
what, from what—because against all rules of ritual,
I, a woman, am here to light this fire. I complete three
circles. I bring the flames down on my father's forehead
glistening with fresh ghee and sandalwood. I know that
at this moment the body catches fire. But, I do not see
this because I have already turned away. I go and sit alone
outside, unaware of season or light. There could be clouds
above, there could be a sharp wind.

After the burning ends, I am handed the ashes in an
earthen pot. The ashes, and that one part of the body that
they say never dies—the navel.

I take this pot of navel and ashes and walk into the pond
by the burning ghat with the family purohit who stands
straight and tall, and never offers me a hand or arm like
the other men do. He tells me to turn my back to the pond

and throw the pot over my shoulders into the water. I do as he tells me. I can hear the sound of the pot cleaving the water in the pond.

How many times will the end come?

Illness

'My eyes,' he said.

She took the towel, dipped it once again in the bowl of iced water, squeezed it, and put it on his eyes. The fever had thinned his face. As it thinned over the days, her love emerged through her hands to hold it. She looked at the hollows beneath his eyes. The hollows were made of circles of bone, soft skin, and a concave darkness. She put her lips there, softly, and his eyes opened.

'My eyes,' he said.

She wet the towel again. On his eyes, and then she travelled the length of his tall, lean body. Through the one large window in the room, she could see the darkness gathering, making even darker his brown body, the smooth stomach, the soft penis, the large feet. She had been doing this for hours, her sari wet with the ice water in places, an ache in her back. Her wrists were small and fragile, but she was not tired, because she did not have a body, only he did.

She dried him, covered him with a fresh white sheet. Outside, small shreds of fading light still remained. She waited and watched till the evening took them all away. Then she lay down next to him, in the bed with its stale fever smell. His eyes were closed. She rested her head. She rested her head in the space between his neck and shoulders, tender dark space, even darker than the room, and gentler than the evening that had just descended.

Gift

I brought my grandmother a gift, a white sari with a border of deep green mangoes in silken thread.

My grandmother was sitting firmly on the floor before a coal oven, making sweets. Shredded coconut, milk and gur were being stirred together to form a thick mixture. She took a lump at a time from this mixture and shaped it with her palms into a small round ball, each one perfect. She was hard at work, the heat from the coal fire bringing forth a layer of moisture on her brow.

'I've brought you a gift,' I said.

'I don't want anything,' she said with a smile.

I laid out before her the stiff tangail sari. She looked at it. She wiped her gur stained hands on the crumpled sari she was wearing and then examined the tangail carefully. 'A fine weave,' she said.

She turned away and began to stir the coconut paste. She took out a lump, rounded it. As she began to make perfect the round shape, holding the sweet in one palm and rolling the other palm over it, a tear came slowly down from one eye.

'What is it?' I said.

'My heart breaks,' said my grandmother, between her tears, 'My heart breaks when one of you brings me a gift.'

Palms

My father, on silent evenings, watched his palms. There were three distinct lines on each palm, etched very deep into the skin, making a pattern of dark brown on beige. On the left hand, the longest one moved in a curve from the top left straight down to the beginning of the wrist, forming a large semi-circle. The second line, beginning from the same source as the first, was also a curve, but smaller, shaped like a fine eyebrow. Far above these two was the third, curving by itself at the top of the palm, right below the fingers. My father looked closely at the lines and the smaller patterns that arose out of them. Then he joined his fingers together so that the tips of the fingers formed one level, unbroken surface. I watched him watching his palms.

When I grew up, unknowingly, I began to watch my own. They looked exactly like his, the same three lines, following the same directions. I too lined up my fingers. When I did this I realised that all the time my father had been looking somewhere else, not at his palms. Perhaps the lines had led him there.

April

It is another April and the mango tree stands, like last year, growing from fullness to greater fullness. This time, new leaves are born continuously, first at the head of the tree, leaves that are rust coloured, slender and long. They are untouched by the thick dust that covers all the older leaves. In a few days the rust changes under the April sun to a new, a fresh green, as if these leaves alone had received a secret shower of rain. Soon they spring forth all over, even further below. These fresh clusters, small but still long and slender, look like rust coloured stars blooming on top of the older leaves. Stirring inside the leaves is a bird never seen before, small and delicate and deep blue.

Underneath the voluminous shade of this mango tree an old man stands. The man is thin, with a long, flowing white beard. On his head is a basket of vegetables, but so few, for the vegetable seller that he must be. There are a few weary pieces of pumpkin and two cucumbers in the basket's vast expanse. Another man comes by, a younger man, reading a letter as he walks. When he comes under the tender shade of the mango tree, he looks up at the leaves that protect him so from the sun. He sits down and reads his long, long letter. The old vegetable seller does not sit, merely waits for a few moments in the shade, holding the basket on top of his head with one arm. He closes his eyes.

This is a new April, more full and ripe than the one that came before. Look, how the sun throws itself in small points of light all over the tree and then disappears into the dark places inside.

Return

Out of the pain, absence and emptiness arises the completely new, the unexpected. The dead person turns slowly, imperceptibly, into a living being again. He leaves behind the past, that season of endings, and enters again the season of change and movement, the present, where his actions can be understood, his face and hands read, his wisdom learnt. Sometimes, when I lean back in my armchair and look right out at the mango tree, my father sits beside me, experiencing the beauty of the evening coming. This has nothing to do with imagination, nothing. The longings disappear in me, the nostalgia of intervening years is dispelled, and what arises from the mists of death is as clear and unsentimental and right as life.

When my father comes we never speak. Sometimes he holds my grown up face in his fatherly palms just to make sure that my load of grief is not more than what I can bear. He always knows what the truth is. With a whole life already lived through, the dead return without doubts. They return pared down, leaner, with the bones more prominent, the eyes larger and more moist, and all their bitterness fallen away forever.

Subcontinent

The subcontinent lies back on the surface of the earth like a man full of abandon, his arms flung out on either side. Above, dark monsoon clouds move in from the ocean and break the back of the hard summer light. On a street like a vein on the subcontinent's body my mother, walking towards her puja room, looks out once at the clouds moving thick and fast and continues on her way.

Alexander of Macedon and his army had never seen rains like this before. Nearchus, Alexander's admiral, told of brass that rained from the sky in brazen drops. The historians call it invention but Nearchus knew what he had seen and heard. In my grandfather's grove, thick with banana trees, the rain fell with the sound of festival dhaks so loud on the broad leaves that he thought it was suddenly the season of harvests, of Durga Pujas, and not the season of rain. It kept him awake for nights.

Alexander's army came to conquer, but had to retreat, surprised, before the vast rivers swollen with rain, rivers like seas that they could not cross without dying.

Alexander's men refused to advance further. They were tired, they lay down their arms. The Greeks returned without vast lands or victory but they returned having seen this singular rain, these rivers, and elephants, and trees with white balls of cotton on them.

In the ancient house of my mother, the dining room ceiling caves in under cover of the sound of thunder. My mother, who ignores natural processes, who has never had a landscape to live by, is forced to turn around and look at the piece of sky above her. The wind comes swirling into her wide open eyes. The rain falls into the bowls of neatly arranged food that she has cooked. It dilutes the yellow dal and floats on the mustard oil that surrounds the vegetables. With the gale in her eyes and the rain above and around her, my mother for once does not think of repair, she thinks of death.

The ancestors gather to watch, my father, my grandfather, the great grandfather who had lost his riches to a tornado wind. Strong boned, quiet faced, liquid eyed, all the generations gather, generations going back to the deltaic lands where they were born, made love, married, died, and coming forward to the time when they fitted their spirits into cities, jostling each other with such innocent expectation and hope gathered in their large eyes, fitting themselves into these spaces of wall and windows, where there was room only for questions, never for answers, and certainly not for a leaping of the heart. This is how time shrinks, say the ancestors as they watch, and becomes as lean and emaciated as a white widow in a falling house. Their ancient hearts, filled with the rhythm of life after life, go out to my mother. Something is coming, thinks my mother, and it is more than the rain.

The Arabs, when they realised the existence of the monsoon winds, began to sail rapidly through the middle of the ocean to the subcontinent, instead of slowly floating along the coasts for months and months as they had done before. The monsoons were benevolent winds, blowing in a north-eastward direction across the Arabian sea in summer, aiding everyone on their way. Traders from the Mediterranean sailed with these winds, bringing on their ships wine, coral, topaz, and most of all, gold, making the subcontinent breathless with opulence. The returning monsoon winds in the winter aided the ships back, ships on which the subcontinent sent spices, jewels, and lions, tigers and elephants for the wild beast shows of Roman emperors.

One whole wall gives way, this time creating its own thunder. It is the middle of the day, but through the space created by the fallen wall my mother can see that it is almost as dark as night. The rain does not fall straight down, but throws itself around in gales before it reaches the ground.

The rain goes on for ten whole days and nights. The streets of the subcontinent flow like rivers. The water runs into houses setting tables and chairs afloat, making quiet the people who sit with their faces in their hands wondering whether this is the same rain they had prayed for, this rain that now brings so much grief. My mother is on the upper floor, but the rain coming in through the broken walls and ceiling floods the house. My mother sits still in that flooding with a stillness suited to summer when nothing moves, but not to this season of the rains when all things become displaced. Inside her there is nothing, no love, no fear, no pain, only an immense emptiness.

When Job Charnock sailed up the river to Sutanutee, he could see nothing but water, the rains falling day and night around him, such rain as he, like Nearchus, had neither heard nor seen before. This was the original rain, before which nothing else had any meaning, and the fine drizzle in his own land seemed an imitation, a smudged, unclear copy.

In this rain filled August when these swamps and marshlands were almost indistinguishable from the river they stood by, where wild animals wandered in the jungles beyond, Charnock had a vision, as keen and sharp as a prophecy. On the banks of the swollen river he moored his boats and men and founded an empire. In this fertile, watery land there sprouted trade and wealth and power. There were grand avenues lit by poignant gas lamps, houses into which the ancestors fitted their spirits. There sprouted the seeds and fruits of new learning unseparated from submission, there was born a child, the last in my riverine family, who would speak her deepest words with the same river lilt but in an alien tongue.

The monsoons float up over the ocean from somewhere below the equator. No one yet knows its reason and its source.

Days have passed and my mother has been watching the rain through the broken ceiling and walls. She has locked the puja room with a brass key, the thirteen small gods floating inside together with dead flowers. As my mother watches the rain she sees a man silently paddling a small boat down the dark water filled street. Something moves inside her, in a remote, speechless place. The next day the fish appear, small and silver. They swim in water that reflects the dark monsoon clouds above, sometimes they float to the surface. They leap high into the cloud filled air and then back into the water again. When the fish come my mother breaks the stillness, she breaks into song, my mother who has never before sung.

'Ei udashi hawar pathe pathe mukul guli jhare …'

On the path of this wistful wind the buds keep falling …

It is a song my father used to love.

After many days the rain eases suddenly and from somewhere behind all this darkness the sun throws a very faint light, no rays, no warmth, just a hue on leaves and trees and houses. The darkness still remains, though touched in places by this faint forefinger of light, creating a sky where everything merges, flows and leaks into the other without a knowledge of sources and endings. It is a sky of great forgiveness.

My mother leaves now her falling house, behind her the
dead ancestors, freed from brick and stone, relieved,
behind her my dead father whose living look of torment
and alarm for her has been replaced by a calm, tender
concern. My mother turns away, forever, from this house.
On the road, filled with water till the waist, boys sail paper
boats, silently. They turn as they see an old woman in a
white sari wading slowly through the dark water. She has
on no blouse, like a village woman, and her sari covers her
thin, old breasts. She passes the monkey man, standing
with monkeys so wet that their fur sticks together in small
clumps. She passes the ragpicker who cannot save his rags
from the rain and has floated his large jute bag on the
water. She passes the bearded ektara player who holds his
ektara close to his chest. She looks at the wanderers she
had never before understood.

The subcontinent bears gently, gently, my mother, in
the crook of its left arm. The monsoon winds come in
from the bay and pass right through her emptiness of
heart, creating a breath of joy that she herself can feel but
not yet understand. There are questions in the eyes of
those who watch her wade by, but not in my mother. The
subcontinent, full of abandon, knows neither repentance

nor mistakes nor redemption, it knows only how to live everything and then put it all behind, seasons and history and geological change. Who can understand what change is? The subcontinent bears gently, gently, my mother, in the crook of its left arm, as deserts are overtaken by forests and flat lands rise slowly into hills.

Embrace

When he wants to hold her, she stands there. 'Come,' he says, and opens his arms. She steps in because he wants her to and because his arms are open. He holds her close to his heart. She keeps her arms hanging at the sides. She feels the hardness of his chest, the side of her face resting on it, her body leaning awkwardly against his, because her arms are at her sides.

She sees outside the blue monsoon light falling without end over everything, up above the not so dark monsoon clouds passing slowly over the sky, down below the mango tree grateful and shining and wet with new rain, the sparrows moving through its branches and leaves. A little girl walks by with bare feet, holding a bottle of milk, tossing her hair back languidly as if she were already a woman. From where does love come, and where does it go, and how does one leave pain behind like a lived, exhausted season?

If she could raise her arms she could regain her balance.

Outside, from the distant minaret, the azaan of dusk comes through the fresh blue light, rising with the long, open syllables of prayer, falling with the short syllables where the muezzin takes his breath. The evening gathers all at once in this season of the monsoons, fading out the leaf clusters on the mango tree. A bird flies straight into the clear glass pane, its small head colliding with the hard surface. It hurts her, but the delicate bird merely wings around, changes its path and flies away over far buildings and trees.

In the farthest things she loses herself, in the closest she assumes definition. She tries to raise her arms and puts them down again.

The evening is complete.

There is no moon this evening, but there are streetlamps standing surprised in the rain, lighting up the flight of a late bird. On the windowpane a lizard eats an insect with clear wings.

She turns away from him, the aanchal of her sari softly brushing his arms, she turns and the earth turns and the lizard over on its back and the leaves in the direction of the rain wind and the rain wind comes up from below the equator and turns sharply to the right with the turning and spinning of the earth.

Ancestors

In my solitude.

The ancestors gather around me sometimes in my solitude. They come when I turn my face halfway back and give the past a transient, loving glance. There is no nostalgia, the heart moves merely at the fact of change. Women come who sat hunched before grinding stones and chopping fish, their saris covering their heads, a sadness or a joy hovering at the edge where the sari met the face. Men come, with a little river mud on their ankles, beneath their white dhotis. The watching generations, sleepless, say they want to sleep, to close their tired eyes.

I come from large, full families of uncles and wives, brothers and cousins, from people near the water, near rivers full with the sweetest fish, where rice grew at the casting of a seed and was endless, and oil was pressed from the yellow mustard seed. They were families from landscapes overrun not only with rivers, but with shining ponds, lakes and streams and when the land grew too hot the rain came in from the bay. Into the water they immersed Durga after the pujas, slaughtered the sacrificial goat at small temples, and lived always amidst the sound of conch shells and ululations and the hiss of frying fish.

Now, there is only myself, living on a breath, not knowing what will come next. I remain without anchor, empty handed, with the street for a friend, and a world constructed from a few simple images. I wait every evening for the first star, the evening star that rises high in the twilight sky before the last streaks of faint crimson have faded, the star that does not tremble.

There are no rivers here, no tall profusion of coconut trees, I tell the ancestors, and the past can never return, while the future carries on in its deeply inevitable way, though unknown to myself. How do I close their sleepless eyes? They look saddened for a moment but the moment passes. Their faces, especially their large, liquid eyes return to their look of endless hope, of a joy merely in wishing that makes fulfillment unnecessary. Their unspoken hopes crowd together inside me, a woman at the end of the line, sitting in her strong spined solitude.

As they leave the darkened room I ask them, did the seers really live, or did people wish them into being with their hopes and griefs and desires? They smile, some with bowed heads so that the smile is only a glow on their foreheads, some with lips pressed together, and some full, looking as straight as light into my questioning eyes. They each offer a different meaning that I cannot grasp, they crane their necks to look out at the growing moon outside my window, especially the women. The white conch-shell bangles and the red ones made of coral tinkle on their arms as they draw their saris closer around their smiles, but they say nothing as they crowd together to leave.

Dust covers all my books and makes them old and yellow before their time.

Imagination

As the boatman rows standing up and as the oars part the clear water, he sings his river song. A sound comes up from his throat long before a bend in the broad river, and fades only once it has been left behind. The subcontinent is the land of long cries.

The boatman has eyes that have turned unclear from always looking around the next far bend, from reading the sky. He never sees precisely what he passes, but people on the banks see him, sometimes shutting his eyes as his throat swells, yet standing steady with his long oars. His long syllabled sounds reach what varied shores, what river lights, what people sitting in memory and yearning on its silent banks, what women pausing in kitchens and turning towards the song as their hearts rise and as they realise the song is neither about love nor death but that it leaves both behind inside them as the boatman rows away.

The river floods in the rains, becomes a sea, bursts its banks and takes over the land. The boatman waits. People wait huddled on the few raised sandbanks where the river has not reached. Cattle flow with the river and drown, trees are felled, and last year's image of Durga sometimes floats to the surface, unrecognisable. People wait with the level, unchanging patience they were born with, they wait without the pretence of will or power. When the flood recedes they walk home with the bottoms of their saris and dhotis dripping wet. The river goes back to itself, leaving the gift of a rich, fertile soil on the land over which people will cast seeds and reap an endless harvest.

The rivers are all imagined. Reality is a fish from the river, gracefully silver. The fishseller begins to scale the fish, rubbing it against the large, curved knife that is fixed onto a wooden stand on the floor. The scales make a soft, grating sound against the knife and fall all silver and perfect around the brown feet of the fishseller. After the scaling the fish is held sideways against the knife and cut through the middle. The red guts are pulled out swiftly with a forefinger and the blood is small and simple, leaving the hands only lightly red. On the silver head, the mouth is open, the pupils of the eyes, large, black and dilated, full of the incredible surprise of death.

My grandfather is leaving the delta lands that are his home.

 SHARMISTHA MOHANTY

Summer

The streets are silent, but dream silent. There is much to speak if only it could be spoken. She watches clay pots and pitchers piled high and quiet, burning earth red in the sun. Inside the pitchers people will fill dark, dark water and when they come home from amazingly hot days they will tip the pitcher halfway to the ground and fill their glasses. They will drink, closing their eyes, thoughtless, remembering nothing.

She walks wearing white, but the fruits, the fruits of summer burst with colour. On these deserted streets she stops to eat a slice of watermelon bought with burning coins that both she and the fruitseller can barely touch. The juice runs down her hands and the sides of her mouth and she throws the now discoloured shell away after she has eaten. It lands on a patch of weeds and mud where the remains of so many fruits decay.

Beggar women sit in abandon on the pavements. Rarely, very rarely, they stretch out a brown palm to a passerby and receive a shining coin. What can one ask for in this scalding summer but for a cool evening that will never come? They put the coin into their cholis where it burns the amazing fullness of their breasts.

A buffalo waits, heavy and inert and as brown as mud. They all wait near solitary trees, these animals, and with such silence in their eyes. There is a horse, sand coloured, with wisps of white mane, so still that not even the memory of a gallop remains. Far beyond is a camel, with its face held high. It stands tied to a mango tree, its large mouth open and its teeth bared, gazing into the distance with its eyes full of pain.

Her grandfather used to sit bare chested on the balcony, as if a part of summer's ripening, the sun directly above his head.

'Don't you feel the heat?' she would ask him.

'It is summer, isn't it?' he would ask her in return. 'In summer there should be heat, desperate heat.'

Only separations bring restraint. To hover always at the window, never to leap, to feel pain but never to come to tears, to talk of living but stay in the realms of what can never be alive. Look, the flowers of summer are insistent, they do not redeem the sun. The fiery orange gulmohur has sprung up all over these trees, and next to it on other trees the golden yellow laburnum. Further on there will be flowers of dark purple.

They say the rains come when the sparrows begin to bathe in the dust.

Gestures

My father holds my face in his hands. It fits so precisely in his large, fatherly palms that all questions take flight.

A man I love holds my face in his long, slender hands and it fits there just as well, my face which is too heavy and full of thoughts to hold in my own two palms. I raise my eyes towards him. It is not just one doubt that falls away as I rest my face, and not only doubts of love.

Sometimes a friend, in passing, in a moment of joy, holds my face and smiles into my eyes. My face always becomes full when it is between another's hands.

Gestures repeat themselves like this, tirelessly. I, a woman, receive that particular one-armed embrace from men, so sudden and strong that it pulls me to them on one side and gathers up my shoulders as I lay my face well below theirs.

The kissing of a hand by a man I have loved for years, for centuries, is yet so unexpected and new, from the hand

spreading to distant places in the blood. The kissing of
a hand by someone not so long known, yet tender in
passing, in the drawing near.

Mistake

Sometimes I mistake everybody for the one I love.

Mourning

On the thirteenth day is when we eat fish again. All this time we have been on a diet of fruits and vegetables. Today is the last day of mourning for my father and the house fills with people. They all join my mother, my aunts and me as we raise the first piece of fish to our mouths. On my banana leaf the old cook puts a large piece, the skin black, the flesh white, and I eat it silently, tasting the fish, savouring the fish, picking out the bones and putting them neatly to one side.

Cities

Most hurtful of all are the sofas. Their deep, original blue is faded almost to grey where peoples' backs and shoulders have rested, for years. The china is always well preserved.

The morning is such a surprise. Can the sun rise here too?

Down empty streets the sound of the rattle drum begins to come closer, joining the sun's insistence. Such beckoning, such hope of the afternoon being lifted off its perpetual hinges. The monkey man arrives, lean faced, and squats on the burning asphalt. His monkeys begin to perform for shut windows, deserted balconies, empty streets. The show finished, the monkey man goes away through winding alleys, rattling his drum which raises again the brown, flat dust of hope. Every day he comes, the monkeys becoming leaner.

People line up with the same asking eyes for milk as for pleasure.

The subcontinent is the land of repetitions, of recurrence.

The cows go to slaughter late at night, parting smoke, winter mist and darkness. They are large, hybrid, disproportionate. Their bodies are vast expanses of grey white flesh, with large, wide bones that form knots in places. The small yellow lights of a bridge shine upon their stupor. This is the hour of tenderness, amazing my fingers on his face.

Only youth, only old age. Never the mellow, the full flavoured, the mature. The seasons pass here with broken backs.

The renouncer, the wanderer. Yes, we had heard of such a man once.

The sun rises, vast, orange and exhausted in the smoke filled dawn.

Standing at the single window in her house of pain, a woman waves.

The back of the neck, below the hairline, is infinitely vulnerable. The spine travels in a hard, crooked line but is full of tenderness, like the shoulder blades that protrude. Arrogance stands protected in front. The back is left hesitant, helpless, completely open to the approaching unknown.

Someone, shrunken and dying in bed, but living on, saying, 'And still the breath doesn't leave the body.' Yet raising a shrunken hand from beneath the impeccable covers to bless, touching the young head, saying, 'May not only your desires be fulfilled, but may you pass beyond the pain of desiring.'

The lamplight falls on trees whose leaves are covered with dust. In complete darkness perhaps something could have been grasped.

Someone, lonely and companionless, stands smiling at the window, because the person on the street below has a companion.

An embrace from behind is love stepping between the back and the unknown.

The eyes of resignation do not open very wide.

When distance is inside, it can no longer be covered
by walking.

When words are stronger than feelings, only then am
I afraid.

Home

In this large house, marriage, birth, celebrations, all have their proper hour, fulfilling every expectation utterly. Never is anyone lonely for too long. Never is anyone empty handed with despair. The face that stays at the window looking at the far sky is pulled back early enough. There are no longings. There are never even the coarse, threadbare saris of unexpected poverty and want. Always the fine, diaphanous garments, the ancient jewellery rich and beautiful on new bridal throats and arms. There is a bordered adolescence, careful marriage and a new bed, there are children and milk flowing in the breasts, and time never too long or too suddenly short. Always, satisfaction comes before desire.

This was a house my grandfather built merely to rest his head, to sleep in when tired, to die in when life ended. That was all.

Then came the sons and daughters of my grandfather. Over the years there were lonely marriages that never found the strength to break, there were born weak, concave children who could not look with fearless eyes at anything. The men left every morning and returned after dark with empty faces, never talking of what they did in their outside hours. There were no solitary moments on sun ravaged afternoons when people sat with their faces in their hands, silent. There was no true grief, or joy or pain. Food was cooked, elaborate food, it was eaten. There were endless rituals, endless hibiscus flowers offered to the gods with a face upturned but restless and ravaged under the skin, the eyelids always moving. There were the gods, the worship, the bringing in of the new year and every ritual the ashes and bones of previous rites from when people lived by the large, winding river and the open fields, every ritual now bearing a curious melancholy, the sense of a lost, spacious past and an even more lost future. There was the sharp, hollow sorrow of not knowing the stagnant from the eternal.

Only death burst through this life, like a song long held in the throat, like the long cry of the ancient boatman in my grandfather's land. Now, eyes that had never been startled with pain showed tears, faces became twisted with sorrow, became swollen, lost shape. The long, black hair of women went uncombed. Death had broken the perfect timing of everything. No matter when, death always came too soon.

Death came, it passed. Life remained, inexorable.

My grandfather saw all of it, this inversion of his understanding of a home, but he loved people. People were so full of need.

Slowly the crows leave for the sky. It is winter and the smoke filled dusk holds only for a few moments. Before the complete darkness of evening comes a deep amber sky against which large trees lean across each other. In the amber light is a face whose form I cannot see clearly. Someone from that home of the past, from a life without strength, without questions, an anchored life without even the hope of movement, yet a life I get drawn towards, unawares, as in a monsoon ocean current, simply because it is the life I once came from, a place without doubts, without the heights and depths of joy and pain, where they are unmoved by the twilight but blow the conch shell and light the incense unfailingly when darkness comes.

Lamp

My grandmother used to say, 'That poor brass lamp, always holding wick and oil and flame, has been serving us ever since you were born.'

What is living and what is not?

Mango Tree

When I watch the mango tree, I do not remember yesterday, and I cannot imagine tomorrow. It is how the leaf clusters tremble today that I see. Today, three brown birds come with thin, fine twigs held in their beaks, today the breeze is strong on the tree, making the birds unsure, restless. As I watch the tree and my sight rests on the diminutive new mangoes that hang from its branches, my face is turned lightly, unknowingly, towards ripening. Otherwise I have forgotten the leaves, the light, the birds of the past and so am not capable of making a future, but what happens that I watch, I wait, for these new mangoes to ripen, craning the neck and the heart? I wait for them to turn golden and become larger than my small palms.

From the light and shadow a storm emerges, a duststorm, which covers the tree with large, coarse particles of dust. The leaves droop under this new weight and the tiny mangoes get hidden underneath. All night the storm ravages the street, the trees, the roofs, without bringing the relief of rain. At dawn the mangoes are all fallen and scattered at the bottom of the tree. Thin, brown legged children come, freshly awake, and take the mangoes away with joy and excitement. No more mangoes appear on the tree, though I wait for days, I watch. The tree remains without fruit, though birds still come, and people still pause in its voluminous shade.

April goes by, the summer passes and the monsoons. The white, light rooms of my solitude cringe in the heat and open up with the rains. Autumn comes, tropical and evanescent, barely a season. All movement is over now, the rising of the heat, the falling of the rains. In the new silence, acceptance comes, not forced, harsh and human, it comes unawares, like a new rust coloured mango leaf above the older ones. I watch, surprised, craning again the neck and the heart, watching the turning of all things, and of the mango tree that turns from a promise of fruit into a tree again.

Terrain

The terrain of illusions is flat.

They lie beside one another in the flat lands, not aware yet of the landscape. The feeling makes her body expansive, her skin pervious. Tears come to her the colour of water, uncommitted. The throat is constricted as the tears come but the body remains untouched. Then, suddenly, the feeling leaps.

She watches as the feeling rises away from them. She becomes only a woman now, full fleshed and ample, nothing more, and he only a symbol of a man. In the flat terrain things have only one dimension, massive and simple. Lying there together, only man and only woman, they are the carcass the feeling leaves behind as it leaps. It circles above them, careful not to touch, to remain pure.

Who knows what passes between them as they lie beside one another? The feeling carries it out of them too soon, transforming it into something large and unrecognisable, insisting by its hovering on naming it as love. It grows, as they watch lying below, and moves out through the one window. It cannot be contained in bodies and rooms.

The feeling glides over the landscape, never touching even here the settling snow, the bare trees, the blowing leaves, but including all of this in its expansiveness, the generosity of something about to die.

In this flat terrain things can go far away and still be seen.

From this distance great longings rise, there is a going towards. At the same time, from this distance, great security settles, there is a staying in. What is too light, like a feeling, floats up and disappears. What is heavy and gravitated like security, remains in place, incapable of movement. But the distance never closes. Things remain very far, and the eye, in order to discern differences, begins to name things.

When the feeling leaves her she becomes insubstantial. There is only the rising away of everything and the being left far and below with a handful of names. Tomorrow, in the cold dawn, she will have to begin again, to become human, to feel the flow of blood, to feel.

The terrain of love comes in curves and spheres.

They lie beside one another, her fingers on his face,
touching shadows and concave places. Not even the roads
outside are flat. In this dark hour of tenderness iron carts
go by on the broken, curving, uneven roads, making
a loud sound of grating metal that fills the night with
a sharpness. The feeling comes. It resides in the space
between two faces that hold each other. It is small and
gracious and giving, it lives between a surrendered head
and the shoulder it rests on, between where a forehead
meets an accepting collarbone. This is its terrain, the
landscape of tenuous, hesitant connections, hollows of
darkness and breath, of skin, bone and curve seen close
through the eyes, everything close to the face, what is far
remaining outside the bounds of the heart till the earth
brings it closer with its turning. Holding the face of the
other, no tears come but the blood turns in the body, slow
and grave, and something more than blood twists so that
it is the body that begins to cry. In this curved, spherical
terrain the body is never spared. A lone crow lets out a
sharp, jet black call that remains pendant in the night as
the feeling settles inside her, to remain and remain and
remain. How it lives, as she holds this face, as it will live
long after, slowly tilling the heart, tilling the words she

uses every day to name things, showing her the world's imprecisions.

The terrain is unending.

It does not remain within the bounds of one being only. The feeling and the body keep turning as on a lathe, becoming sharpened, sharpened, shaped. Because of the turning distances close and change, everywhere. There are endless faces of men and women, coming towards, going away, different geographies with their own centres of pain, new slants of morning light by the sea and in cities. From the holding of one face the world begins to revolve, as on an axis, taking her through the terrain of imperfections, of resistances. Look, there is a woman frying fish as the twilight deepens, with something unfulfilled in her moving hands. There is a man with a lean face who does not know what a feeling is. And there is a man with the slowly healing wound of separation inside him, whimpering like an animal in the darkness of his heart. The feeling is always inside her, never planting, only tilling, keeping her in movement, in small, deep turnings over.

Watching

The sudden undertow of that which must be left behind.

Ahead, the uncertainty of mountains, the hesitant seas.

The body, incapable of abandon or surrender. The body, full of repetitions.

At the end of every life, there is a house. At the end of every house, moss, soft and deep.

Under the mature moon, completeness. Only completeness can throw patterns of such light on streets and trees and rivers.

Under the evening sky, on an open terrace, a boy sits by a yellow lamp, reading. The large pool of light falls over him and gathers him in, as he reads about mountains and monuments he will never see. Near him, out of the light, where the stars float above, two women bend their heads in prayer and raise them up again, eyes closed to the open, drifting summer sky.

When everything has its place, the distances between things remain unchanged.

Always the river on the edges, lonely, abandoned, barely flowing, longing to assume the street's dark face.

The level of sorrow rises just a little, like water, and sways gently from side to side before settling again.

A blue, relentless sky hangs over the tropical earth at all times. It is because of this that people wait with such infinite patience for the rains. Only under dark, moving clouds can the eyes open wide and travel far.

The street bares all its wounds, the broken sidewalks, the gaping insides of asphalt. It no longer needs to exercise caution. In the darkness, under the broken lamplight, it is the street that assuages, so the walker can somehow pass over it.

Small green moths come in these dark evenings to hover and then die around my face in the yellow lamplight.

In faces that ask, both avidity and resignation in equal measure, unseparated, flowing into one another. The asking tainted with helpless resignation, the acceptance inundated by avidity.

On these flat roofs, open to the sky, pigeons and forgetting reside.

'My love, my love,' he said. He woke her gently in the summer night. 'My love,' he said, 'it's me.'

To stand still, not to sway, or swerve, or begin to walk away.

Continental Drift

When the storm came, sudden and dark, a woman's ohrni flew back, curved outward, billowing like a sail on a dark monsoon sea, and flew away from the arms she raised to gather it around her. It was possible for the ohrni and the cloud to come closer to one another. The subcontinent is the land of long cries.

The subcontinent was once part of a great land mass, sharing common boundaries with Africa, Antarctica and Australia. Almost one hundred and twenty million years ago it broke away and began its long, long journey towards Asia.

The azaan, the twilight and the birds all rise together. Who knows where they will fall?

Now that the rivers are far, they sail and sing on the blackened streets. The monkey man with his rattle drum, the seller of fish and fruits, the cotton workman with balls of cotton in a jute bag over his always bent shoulders, the man with white jasmines falling from his hands when evening comes. Sometimes there may be songs, but more often there are sounds, of words repeated, attenuated, rarefied, becoming a cry from the heart that earns, and a cry for earning that takes the heart along its endless way.

In this geography, where is necessity located? In places not yet understood, or places long forgotten?

My grandfather is leaving the river lands that are his home. Beneath his white dhoti there is a little river mud on his strong ankles.

Her body was free of clothing, but the head was still covered by her ohrni. In the making of love it had slipped back to the middle of her head. It curved in near the ears and softly reached out at her face, then fell over her neck and shoulders. Beyond that she was no longer aware of its existence, though it fell in a fine sheath away, away from her breasts, over her long, black hair, down her bare back to the floor.

The subcontinent covered six thousand kilometres on the ancient Tethys Sea between the land it had left and the land it was travelling towards. As it came closer to Asia, an island arc of volcanoes rose up from the sea ahead of it. The subcontinent and this arc of volcanoes together collided with the Asian land mass. From the force of this collision the Himalayas rose up towards the sky.

The sky of joy has no centre, and without reason, covers everything.

In the subcontinent, the depths are thrown up by destiny. The wave stretches out on a mountaintop, and flows over.

There is no place here for the short, broken feeling.

This is a time of quietude above. There are unseen agonies deep beneath, unknown fragilities. One may emerge a mountain range or an endless lake.

The whitewashed thresholds are full of love, and over them the mango leaves hang in silence, every curl on the leaves firm and unchangeable.

Relationship is everywhere and the threshold is always for entrances.

Bacteria emerge from the depths of the earth and diseases live, yellow and full like jaundice. Everything lives and everything comes in, fluttering sparrows and silent

lizards, soft eyed cattle and wanderers, dust and the rain
that washes it away.

Throats and rain, beaks and sky and rattle drums, the
long cry has many beginnings. The endings are always
unknown.

In the still and unforgiving heat of afternoon, the heart
is thrown back on itself. After sunset it is joined by the
insistent cicadas and the silent fireflies.

On cremation's pyre, a body burns, blackening. In the sky,
the sun rages. The fire below and the fire above become
one long cry and travel through the sky together to
unknown distances, to spaces incapable of closure.

The body, supple and agile, capable of bending forward
with love, with a deep admiration. The body, bending,
bowing, lowering itself, gathering in, always knowing its
place, yet always crossing its own boundaries.

After every lovemaking, a woman gathered up her ohrni,
bringing it back to the point where the line of her hair
ended and her soft skin began.

After the collision the subcontinent rotated
anticlockwise, joining firmly with Asia, slamming shut
like a door, closing and erasing the sea that had covered
the space between. All that had been coastline where
the joining took place, now turned into high valleys,
mountains and hills. The rocks and cliff faces here still
have the imprint of sea waves. This is the longest cry of all.

Jamdani

The jamdani saris of the northern plains are made of the finest, lightest cotton and woven in shades of white. In the unforgiving summer of the north even a hint of colour may be too extravagant. The summer sun has ripened over these plains for the longest time, drying up the rivers to a thin line in a sad channel, it has opened up the dead earth in thick, destitute cracks and raised dust that is thick and coarse and everlasting. The trees still offer a weakened shade, but the leaves are brown with dust that never falls away.

The life preserving jamdani unravels the most delicate nuances of white. When the inexorable sun shines through the fabric there can be seen the whiteness of a rain spent autumn cloud, the purity of white sandalwood, the brightness of an autumn moon that is never shadowed over. Through these tones of white are woven flowers, birds, trees and moons, a more graceful and compassionate earth.

When the sun finally sets on the plains, it is only a small reprieve. People wait through the still, unbearable evening for a small fragment of a breeze. When the breeze comes, so short, so sharply transient, so indifferent to human suffering, it is the flowers and the birds on the jamdani that flutter first, and then the heart.

Is it only the mystics who can wear rags and make them whole?

Tropics

The damp, fertile heart sometimes forgets everything.

The damp, fertile heart goes out to old men feeling left
behind in their light, fluttering dhotis; to men who lean
from balconies where leaves sprout from the stones;
to men whose hands raise food from old, dented
kansa plates.

The damp, fertile heart is sometimes covered over with
the softest moss.

The damp, fertile heart can stand its ground against all
that calls itself new. Only sometimes it moves under the
afternoon shade of a great tree and falls asleep.

The damp, fertile heart has many destinies. Of
destinations it knows nothing at all.

The damp, fertile heart understands the breaking down as
well as the living.

The damp, fertile heart never changes landscapes.

The damp, fertile heart is awake when everything else sleeps. The koel calls on it in the complete darkness of dawn.

The damp, fertile heart turns hesitant only at the approach of the truly new. It knows that this is when anything can happen.

Fabric

The cosmos is one continuous fabric, woven on a loom, a grid pattern created by the warp and woof. There is an integrity in the uncut garment, the sari and dhoti, in the cloth that is woven as one piece. Objects and actions have many meanings, many, many possibilities, and are always moving to fulfil them. At twilight the incense is taken through every darkening room, the lamps are lit and the conch shell blown to keep away insects and creatures of harm, and also to welcome the evening, to celebrate its constant coming. When nothing is only itself, separations cease, the world is lived as one continuous landscape, with its monsoons, deserts and trees; with ripening paddy fields, fluttering, uncut saris and anchored homes; with oil lamps, love and grief. The tireless fire burns for weddings and pyres, worship and sacrifices, and in kitchens, cooking every day's quiet food. The self carries the knowledge of being uncut from the world's landscape, but it cannot always yield. It knows how to take a deep breath, to change always, to flow, it knows that borders are the mind's fear only. The soul is not this, not that; it is unseizable for it cannot be seized; is unbound, does not tremble. It is only the mystics who can wear rags and make them whole.

It has been difficult to reconstruct the subcontinent's past because its dead were never buried. The fire of death ends in air. Other lands had rocks and stones.

The temple is full of the sound of heavy, ancient bells. People crowd and huddle together, walking with their bare feet on the muddied, hot stone.

They pass through large halls supported by granite columns a thousand years old, each one carved differently, each one indescribable in its intricacy. They press further in, crossing doorways and thresholds, leaving the light of the sun further away. It becomes darker and small oil lamps begin to burn, there are no windows, not even a small opening for sunlight. The doors become smaller so people must crouch and bend to go through, though the hunchbacked, and those doubled over with age, and children, do not notice this. Finally, they arrive at the smallest chamber of all where the dark, granite face of god lies in wait, lit unevenly by an oil lamp. They stand there, holding flowers with extravagant stamens and imploring colours.

They ask, ask, ask, they gaze at the granite face, they shut their eyes with hope.

There are only these few moments before others press in insistently from behind. They start to move again and this time the journey of muddied feet is from darkness to light. The hot, sunlit stone in the temple courtyard scorches the soles. That was the place of moorings, this is the moving world.

It becomes difficult. What the heart knows and what it lives begin to separate. There is the deep desire to deny that the heart finds its rest only in movement, in turnings, in mergings, in twilights of change.

Forest

It is night in the forests of the self, night without stars. The low, dark sky touches the mango and peepul trees, bends over their ripening fruit, curves into points with their leaves. Walking is difficult under this sky, in the moon's absence, the limbs are lost and it is only the face that moves ahead. The silence of the forest, the silence. It stills even the unquiet heart. Only the breath remains. Outside, the world's onward movement, unfathomable. Inside the forest, a dispersed heart, gathering itself.

Words awaken in the forest, one by one. Everything here is insubstantial, unspeakable, and the word is freed from its purpose. Full of abandon, each word reveals its many truths.

Deep inside the forest a river flows, only a shade lighter than the dark sky above it. On the banks of the river, in a grove of mango trees, there are traces of a quiet light. In a clearing on the forest floor, on a bed of mango and peepul leaves and roots, Krishna's beseeching blue body leans over Radha's answering wheat coloured form. Radha's long hair flows away from her head, in the direction of the flowing river, and Krishna's falls over his bare blue back. The increased light is from the jewels on Krishna's head, it makes their bodies luminous.

Krishna half sits, his legs parted, over Radha. She has separated her legs for him, they rest on either side of Krishna's body. Everything is open and bared, the legs, the arms, the breasts, the eyes.

There is a gaze in which the eyes do not close for a long, long time. At the end, the eyelid drops very slowly, like a breath, and rises anew. The gaze rests beyond things, or between them. It lives in the empty spaces created by the world's eternal movement. The other world is very close, it hangs low, at an angle, over this one.

The walk out of the forest is no less difficult than the walking in. Inside the room there is the stillness of the whole forest, the stillness. Perhaps in the evening the wind will blow, will blow. A ripe mango will detach itself from its branch and fall with a sudden sound on the moss covered paving below. Dried mango leaves will move like approaching footsteps on the stone. The uprooted home will never again settle, never again settle.

Star

The stillness of the heart is everything in the face of pain. This is where the star and the trembling go their separate ways.

Mountain

The mountains are very different from the plains.

From the plains the land bursts free and rises upwards, leaving deep, open spaces as it rises. A river of unknown beginnings flows through these narrow gorges, as white as milk, gradually becoming transparent as it reaches the plains, thicker and more muddy across the flat lands as it travels to the bay. Going up to the mountains the road bends and curves always along the course of this river, a flowing companion. There are rare birds whose calls hang solitary in the clear, thin air, and fragile mountain flowers, small and pale coloured, the most unpretentious roots and grasses, and tall trees of evergreen and pine. There is water springing from rocks and crevices, falling abundantly into open palms, or on to a face raised upwards. Looking ahead and up there is the summit of the mountains, the highest in the world. The sun is at once fine and strong, looking light and clear but burning the skin unawares. This is a landscape of the turning face, where the eyes and the face want to accept everything. The rocks, the water, the flowers, are still personal here, standing close, brushing against the neck and shoulders, never turning away, taking care.

It is like this for so long, for days, that nothing else can any longer be imagined. The road, though relentless, is kind, and unravels change at the slowest pace, always patient, protecting. Sometimes a fluttering, concerned woodpecker leads the way.

When is it that the woodpecker disappears, and even the grey pigeon, the unassuming sparrow? At about the same time the turning face looks for flowers, even the smallest, and finds none. Not one, even hidden under a rock or boulder. Soon, the trees begin to disappear, first the evergreen, then the pine. The road becomes impatient, perhaps revealing too much, warning the face which now knows only to hold still and look straight ahead. Sometimes, when the eyes find a sprig or leaves bursting forth from a crevice, there arises an affection as from the oldest of life's bonds.

Ahead rise the peaks of the mountains. Everything is white, the rocks, the road, the sky. Down in the gorge the river suddenly seems more distant, retracted, keeping to itself.

When the road ends the face is somewhere barely below a
sky full of clarity, whether in sunlight or in countless stars,
surrounded by mountain peaks where no roads yet go.
The river hardly flows here through the barren, massive
mountain sides, and is cold and flat over low lying stones.

This is the landscape of indifference, bestowing nothing.
The self is silenced by this austerity, stilled by this
overwhelming fate. The memory of the sea seems a
comfort here, the waves that move so full of compassion
and fall on the shore, the tides of consideration, the fish
that can be held in one's hands, touched, the shells that
remain forever.

There is movement here too. The sun rises and sets. The
moon arcs across the sky.

Slowly, everything becomes past, what has already
happened, gone. No memories exist to be recalled. The
face can turn nowhere but to this austere present, it looks
down at the ground so barren and covered with stones.
Loneliness enters the body and heart, inexpressible in
its completeness. Then fear comes, unable to hide here
even in the night, found out always by a moon almost as
luminous as the sun. With nowhere to hide and nothing

     SHARMISTHA MOHANTY

to hold, the body can perform only one action. It goes
down on its knees.

What else can the body do before these indifferent, bare
mountains, before the sharp, sorrowful things that rise
inside the self and will not move, will make themselves
acknowledged. And there is no going further.

To travel far beyond the personal, to travel towards the
anonymous, to what cannot be possessed.

Solitude

I do not know what impels me in these white, light solitary rooms. There is a reed mat, smooth and luminous, on which I lie. If I fall asleep on my side the weave of the mat leaves a pattern on my face. There is a table and a lamp for the night, a mango tree by day, and my soft, crumpled sari always. The sari can contain everything, the body and what rises from inside it. There is nothing else in these bare rooms and when someone comes they fill all of this to the brim. From inside my solitude every person seems larger than life and I open wide my eyes to look at them. They sit near the windows. If it is evening I ask them to sit facing the solitary moon, if it is day they sit beside the mango tree. When their eyes soften before these things I smile as if the tree, the sky, were mine. I love what is fact, I love what cannot be denied. When someone leaves my rooms of solitude they leave a voice behind, or two fluttering hands, so that even after they have left I will not be without companion. Perhaps they know that solitude sometimes breaks down into loneliness and returns, very slowly, to solitude again.

The sky is the colour of a sparrow's wings. The duststorm
of summer's rage arrives and enters here all at once.
There is dust on my feet and hands, on my unprotected
lips. Outside, the leaves of the mango tree turn to brown
and there is not a single bird on its profuse branches.
Sometimes at summer's peak comes a tiredness neither
sky nor birds nor leaves nor a companion can ease.
The storm keeps swirling and moving, ahead of itself,
throwing more coarse dust into the rooms. I never close
these windows, they are for entrances and for reflection.

After the storm the rain comes and the tiredness lifts.
It comes in small, liquid stars and begins to wash away
the dust inside. What is there for me to do? I do not
know what happens in other geographies, but this is a
tropical solitude and there is nothing that does not come
in. Voices and cries, the tadpole that takes shelter here
before the rains, a wayward butterfly. On a still afternoon,
walking down the stairs, I disturb the sparrows, their
chirping and their quiet lines of flight. At midnight,
waking suddenly, there is the auspicious white owl,
perched on a lamp, steadily watching the darkness.
What borders, what exclusion? My solitude fills up,
becomes rounded, and turns every day, a small, small,
earth, furrowed by everything that comes this way. There

is always the koel before dawn, through the night the deep, serious bellowing of cattle, the long cry of ducks in scattered, lonely ponds.

The fish are small, the size of her palms, and black-skinned—koi fish. They lie submerged in bowls of water in the kitchen. Suddenly, one jumps out, makes an arc in the air and falls to the floor. It moves, writhes, and then lies still. She picks up the fish in her two hands and returns it to the bowl. When a very old person refused to submit to death, her grandmother would say, 'He has the spirit of a koi fish.'

When the fish are all finally still, she prepares them for cooking. She takes their firm black bodies in her hand and rubs them with salt and holud. Then she heats the pungent mustard oil in the pan till it begins to smoke. No matter where she is, the oil must always be from mustard, the only one in which to cook this sweet water fish from a deltaic land. When the oil begins to smoke she puts the fish in one by one, carefully, so the oil does not splutter very much as it makes contact with the fish. As the oil rages and hisses she must keep turning the fish over

　　　　SHARMISTHA MOHANTY

rapidly so that the skin does not begin to peel off. This is
a knowledge that has come through generations and it
comes to her without effort, with grace. She loves what has
lived long, she loves what can be passed down.

Outside the large windows it is twilight. The crows make
circles in this sky, a twilight ritual. Their cries are not
elongated and sorrowful as in the sun ravaged afternoon,
but short now, and upward rising. The fish are fried and
still and she takes them out of the pan. Later she will put
them in a gravy that she will cook after darkness comes. In
this indulgent twilight she can do nothing. Slowly, the sky
turns black, the same colour as the crows, as the fish she
has been cooking. The twilight deepens and reaches that
point when almost everything is dark but a soft light still
remains, the last point before evening is made definite.
It is for her the ineffable time, that comes each day then
passes, turning everything over in its leaving.

In solitude.

In solitude everything falls away. Womanhood, the places
already left, the places to come, the dead, all those who

have been loved, and all those the future may bring. The white, light rooms carry nothing except a slant of morning sunlight on the straw weave. Solitude comes, making expansive the body and heart, so that all things may pass through, choiceless. In the end, this solitude belongs to no one, it has travelled far outside any being, become nameless, undefinable.

Through the self everything comes, from the self everything falls away.

———◇———

Acknowledgements

The first limited edition of *Book One* was made possible by
Mani Kaul and Udayan Patel
and
Kuntal Bhogilal
Nita Bhogilal
Merind India
Mandira Mitra
Dr P.K. Mohanty
Sarvadaman Ray
Jyotsna Shekhar
Asha Sheth
Xal-Praxis Foundation

Thank you very much
Sudarshan Shetty
Dayanita Singh
Amardeep Behl
Sunita Paul
Yogesh Rawal

Excerpts from *Book One* have appeared in *Indian Literature,*
The Granta Book of New Writing, and the catalogue for Paper
Moon, a solo show by the visual artist Sudarshan Shetty.

Formations

A faith like an axe. As heavy, as light.

– Franz Kafka

Book One was my very first work. I was a fiction writer and had graduated some years ago with an MFA in fiction from the Iowa Writers' Workshop. I did not yet see myself as a poet. After attempts at short stories which were realist narratives I felt I needed a different path. I wanted a way that took me straight to the condensation and immediate depth of poetry, while remaining within prose, and a way that had movement and saturation at the same time. The tentative answer seemed to be in composing through brief sections that were related. The form of *Book One* emerged as I began to write and I saw that the form could not be linear, its growth would be from the centre outward, slowly forming a whole. To help achieve this I also wanted to work with a certain distillation of language the way poets did.

Book One was seeded from the coming together of all these elements.

I composed the book with the human and the non-human equally in my consciousness, without hierarchy. I did not think of foreground or background, each thing had its own place. I composed with light, a person, a tree, a landscape, a ritual. The biographical and the non-biographical emerged with equal force.

As I wrote, the connections between things, over them, around them, beneath them, began to show, and each element gave off its texture and feeling and form, till they no longer remained grounded in their own particularities. As if they were not people or things, but formations, breathing their own breath, in a landscape of continuity.

In this continuous landscape things recurred and returned—people, rituals, the subcontinent. Each time the attempt was to explore a new aspect of what had returned. The book's unity emerged partly from this and partly from the nature of the gaze, a tone and a voice, the writer's disposition.

The writers who were very important to me at the time, and still are, and from whom I received the most, were Marcel Proust with his singular dilation of time and memory; Hermann Broch, whose *The Death of Virgil,* a 'novel' of five hundred pages, has been called a prose poem; Juan Rulfo, who wrote of the living and the dead in the same tone and without referring to past and present; Virginia Woolf in *The Waves,* building up her characters only through their inner worlds; Rainer Maria Rilke in *The Notebooks of Malte Laurids Brigge,* a 'novel' which took the form of a diary, fragmented and divergent but always seeing into people and things.

They were all writers for whom plot was not important nor the psychological building of a character. Each one of them had a singular style and language and vision. They transformed, radically, the art of the classical novel.

I was also reading the great poets René Char, Rilke, Walt Whitman, alongside the Bhakti poets and Chinese classical poetry.

Book One turned out to be crucial in the formation of my own ideas. Since then I have almost never worked with a given form. Each time it is a discovery and one begins in a precarious position, entirely in the unknown.

There are wounds that I write from, wounds that are impossible to heal, that may be rooted in my own circumstances and self but have taken on a life of their own, or are wounds that have always existed without any cause. And the tone and texture of one's work is a response to that, in some inexplicable way, and each work is an impossible attempt at wholeness.

The only problem that arose then was in 'naming' *Book One*. Was it poetry or a novel? If a novel, why did it not have a plot? At the time I was also in conversation with my mentor at the Iowa Writers' Workshop, the great writer James Alan McPherson, and with the filmmaker Mani Kaul. They had both, in their own way, been moving away from the realist narrative form. They strengthened my conviction in a unity that did not come from plot and that the novel could go in any direction that its writer wanted it to go. In the end I decided to call it a novel.

Perhaps we in India are excessively under the influence of the English or American realist tradition. Latin America and Europe, for example, have taken the novel in many other, very rich, directions. How does the novel remain a mode of discovery? If literature is to be a quest for understanding the self and its world it must have multiple ways of being, endless possibilities.

The problem of genre, I have found, is not a problem that stops readers, it is a problem of a market anxious to name things, it is a problem for most publishers who are apprehensive about selling a work outside a known genre. But over the years I have seen that *readers* of this book rarely have a problem with the 'form'.

Today, I no longer think of *Book One* as a novel. I don't feel the need to name it. Perhaps these are connected prose poems or prose texts that form a whole.

There is too much of the rational in our world. Poetry and fiction give voice to things outside it. And the opposite of the word rational is not irrational, it is imagination and poetic truth, a truth which is always provisional, but which allows us to live more completely.

I remember Tukaram:

'We are here
To reveal
We do not waste
Words.'

Afterword

This book was written more than three decades ago and brought out as a limited edition in 1995. *Book One* had done the rounds of publishers abroad and in India, but was found too experimental and lacking in 'narrative'.

My husband Kabir Mohanty, a filmmaker and video artist, was insistent that we should bring out the book ourselves. We took some months to think this over.

At the time I had recently met the profound film director Mani Kaul and had worked with him on the screenplay of his film *Nazar*. I was living in Calcutta and called up Mani to ask for his advice. He had read the manuscript some months ago and found it very worthy. 'Come to Bombay,' he said, 'and we will find a way.' So I got on a train and went to Bombay.

In Bombay, he brought the problem to a friend, the psychoanalyst Udayan Patel whom I had also met recently. They both thought about the book and suggested we all raise money and publish it. We began to ask friends, foundations and family. The names of those who contributed are listed at the back of this edition.

It was suggested that Delhi was the place to have the book printed. I had chosen the cover of the book—a quiet and moving etching by the artist Yogesh Rawal. Yogesh had very kindly allowed me to use it, for a nominal fee. My husband and I did a hunt for the paper and found white Pune handmade paper for the cover. A dear friend, the artist Sudarshan Shetty, helped me with reproducing the etching. The ace printer Sunita Paul printed it for us at Paul's Press. We did five hundred copies and I handwrote the title in black ink on the cover and the spine, with a fountain pen. My friend Nalin Pandya, the filmmaker, bought the very first copy. It was priced at Rs 300.

Once the book was printed and ready I came back to Bombay and called Dom Moraes. I wanted to give him a copy. He told me he did not want any more books from anyone and had no time to read them. I decided to go to his flat in Colaba, ring the bell, and hand it to whoever opened the door. I left it with his housekeeper, Shubham, and asked him to give it to Dom. I also left my friend's telephone number in the envelope, just in case. I didn't expect to hear back.

The next evening the phone rang and it was Dom. He had finished reading it already and thought it was a very original voice. He invited me to tea and was very kind. He asked me about the work, about myself, and I didn't realise it was partly an interview till a photographer came. He then said he was writing on the book for *Mid-Day*.

That was the first public review and discussion of *Book One*. Several papers and magazines reviewed it after that.

Then came the readings. The very first reading was on the lawns of Ashok Nag's home in Calcutta. He was a childhood friend. Naveen Kishore and Anjum Katyal of Seagull Books helped spread the word and Naveen reviewed the book.

The second one was in Bombay. I was looking for a good venue for the reading. It was, in those days, not easy to find. Sudarshan Shetty had just opened his first solo show *Paper Moon,* at a place called Framjee Cowasjee Hall opposite the Metro Cinema. He said, 'Why don't you do it at my exhibition?' I said, 'But how? Your sculptures are there!' He said, 'We'll push them to the side and make space in the middle.' It was, and remains for me to this day, a singularly generous and moving offer. And that's

what we did. The place was large enough and I read, I
remember, with Sudarshan Shetty's unforgettable horse
with its hooves on a boat, a miniature house on its back,
looking over us. I remember the reading was attended
by about fifty people. Dom came too, towards the end.
Outside, Ribhu Kaul, Mani's very young son, sold copies of
the book.

In Bangalore, my friend Sharath Ananthamurthy organised
a reading at the Sahitya Akademi after which he arranged
a very lively gathering at his home. P. Lankesh invited me
to do a reading sponsored by his *Lankesh Patrike*, which
gave me the opportunity to read to Kannada writers and
readers, not just English language ones. I remember that
whiskey, rum and vodka were served during the reading.
There was an intense discussion afterwards.

I remember that Arvind Krishna Mehrotra, whom I met
for the first time in Bombay right after *Book One* came out,
and Adil Jussawalla were very supportive and spread the
word about the book.

There were other readings, word got around and the copies
did sell out over time. I approached T.N. Shanbhag of the
now gone Strand Book Stall in Bombay to stock copies. He

immediately took ten copies and gave me the full amount up front, a very rare gesture that perhaps only he was capable of.

So many years later, I gave one of the last remaining copies to publisher Karthika V.K., who had published my most recent work, *Extinctions*. I was apprehensive, but she very quickly said she wanted to publish it. I am very grateful to her for the new life she has given to *Book One*.

September 2023

Index

Feb 28/93

Dear Shanmishtha

 I shall put down in this letter
what I was trying to explain on
the phone.
      It was useful to have gone
through the novel in a single
sitting of three hours : 7.00 PM
to 10 PM. While I read on
the evening turned into night
 I discovered that your novel
needs that sort of change
in light as rhythms undergo
a sea change by the time
the unfolding comes to an end.
you should certainly 'prohibit'
readers from picking up the
book in late mornings. or after
lunch or worse sit and,
read in a room 'illuminated' by
tube-lights .

The beginning appears to be
preoccupied with ~~both~~ horizontal
movements , with descriptions
that spread that way. The rhythms are
~~so~~ slow. Your language is
untouched by metaphors but
I ~~do~~ feel that slow rhythms need ~~to~~
not resort to ~~certain~~ 'poetic'
ethos that borders on the
metaphorical. It ~~is in fact~~
could be an attempt to
sustain the feeling of movement
the most essential component
in any non-narrative enterprise *
In the narrative forms 'the
life and times' of characters
create(s) the illusion of (historical)
movement, whereas the
non-narrative is always freed

* A slow rhythm
may collapse

...ith creating a moving experience
emotions that are 'documentary'

I am able to make
is observation because the
novel already contains ~~the~~ a
strength of true simplicity, profound
feeling and an extraordinary
respect anything living. Or ^can deed
shall I say? [I really am most
enamoured of your writing]

This difficulty disappears
the ~~that~~ what I imagine as
the first movement ^finishes, the second
shifts to what can be termed
as the verticals. These ascend
and descend upon the horizontal
spread. You must have a keen
musical hand to have organised
these intensive movements (in and
out) with such clarity that they
~~do not~~ ^never overlap confusedly

The right overlapping or shall we
say a simultaneity of all the
three movements occurs in the
last, the third movement. It
calls forth for a ^wider participation
of that ^we may call nature
(including the one that is human)
Nothing distinguishes ^itself on the ~~basis~~
account of its hierarchical
position.

I hope its useful to
read this letter. If not just
forget these friendly remarks
and continue with the great
work you have engaged
yourself in.

My best wishes.

Affectionately Yours

Mani

P.

The question: what is it
that sustains a slow rhythm
which moves without clear
accents? A tidal wave
for instance, recurs without a
~~any~~ metrical rhythm. There
are no points ~~of stress~~ that
that become predictable
points of stress. Your work
is a series of poems. Doubtless.
But its also a novel!
I think it need not be
'poetic' and in the same ~~way~~ way
it need not be 'narrative'
It is ^a nunction — in the
sense how everything, every word
appears to nuncte.

More when we meet

About the Author

Sharmistha Mohanty is the author of three works of prose, *Book One*, *New Life* and *Five Movements in Praise*. Her work pushes the boundaries of fictional prose, moving it towards the prose poem. Mohanty's writing has been deeply impacted by the varied pasts of India, especially the most remote, and her work claims these pasts as contemporary, as a belief in time being untamed. Her writing holds the past and the now and the experimental equally, where varied elements move towards or away from each other with great velocity and every compositional framework is created anew. *The Gods Came Afterwards*, a book of poems, was published in 2019, followed by *Extinctions*, a book of prose poems that appeared in August 2022.

She has also translated a selection of Tagore's fiction, *Broken Nest and Other Stories*.

Five Movements in Praise has been translated into Spanish and will appear in Argentina and Chile in early 2024.

A chapbook made from a selection of poems from
The Gods Came Afterwards appeared in early 2020 from
Ediciones Pen Presse in Spanish. The poems are translated
by the acclaimed Argentinian poet Mercedes Roffe.

Her work has been published in several journals across
the world including *Poetry, Granta, World Literature Today,
The New Statesman* and the Chinese *Jintian*.

Mohanty is the founder-editor of the online literature
journal *Almost Island* (www.almostisland.com). and
the initiator of the Almost Island Dialogues, an annual
international writers gathering held in New Delhi, both
in existence for fifteen years. Almost Island has also
published books and has till date done six, including both
poetry and prose.

Mohanty was invited to be on the International Faculty
for the Creative Writing MFA at the City University of
Hong Kong, where she taught from 2010 to 2016. She has
also taught at the Creative Writing programme at Naropa
University, set up by Allen Ginsberg.

She has held fellowships at the Akademie Schloss Solitude
in Germany, at Ledig House in New York, had residencies

at the La Napoule Foundation for the Arts in France, and Yaddo, USA, 2009. Mohanty is a recipient of a Senior Fellowship from the Indian Ministry of Culture.

She was a participant in the Kochi Muziris Biennale, the largest art biennale in Asia (December 2016–March 2017), where she created a poetry, light and sound installation *I Make New the Song Born of Old.*

Mohanty has had a deep involvement with the serious Indian cinema. She has worked and interacted with some of its finest practitioners—directors, cinematographers, editors and sound designers. Mohanty wrote the script for *Nazar*, working with the great director Mani Kaul, with whom she had an ongoing dialogue for over twenty years till his death in 2011.

She has also been nurtured in her work by an immersion in the artistic traditions of India's past, which includes being a student of *Dhrupad*—the oldest form of Indian classical music—under Bahauddin Dagar.

She lives in Mumbai with her husband Kabir Mohanty, a filmmaker and video artist.